10-7-07
Dear Anna,
Heb. 11:1
Kenneth

Faith
can move
MOUNTAINS

KENNETH McGEE

TATE PUBLISHING, LLC

TABLE OF CONTENTS

FOREWORD

"Faith Can Move Mountains," is not just another book on faith. It is a journey with *faith!* You will read life-changing stories that will be both uplifting and encouraging. It is one thing to read a book on faith, and quite another thing to experience the *power of faith*. You will find this book to be difficult to put down as page after page of God's miraculous power is unveiled. You will truly discover when the final chapter is completed that, "Faith Can Move Mountains."

Jim McNabb

Senior Pastor–"The Bridge,"
formerly, Mustang Assembly of God
Assistant District Superintendent of the
Oklahoma District of the Assemblies of God

INTRODUCTION

F-a-i-t-h . . . only five letters of the alphabet . . . but in the assembly of these letters we have the most powerful word in the English language! Webster's dictionary gives us the theological definition of faith as: "That trust in God and in His promises as made through Christ, by which man is saved." **Matthew 17:20** reads, **"And Jesus said unto them, Because of your unbelief: for verily I say unto you, If ye have faith as a grain of mustard seed, ye shall say unto this mountain, Remove hence to yonder place; and it shall remove; and nothing shall be impossible unto you."** The last line of this scripture holds a promise that has no bounds for those who believe in Christ.

It is my sincere desire that the message contained in this book will strengthen your faith in a Christ who is alive today; one who is still **" . . . able to do exceeding abundantly above all that we can ask or think, according to the power that worketh in us," Ephesians 3:20.**

Early in my ministry the Lord gave me a song which I entitled "Faith Can Move Mountains." Gretnia and I were returning from a revival meeting at Glad Tidings Assembly of God in Oklahoma City. As we were driving home that night, the Lord began giving me the words to the song. I told Gretnia to get something on which to write. The church had given us a grocery pounding as an offering that night so we had a number of cardboard boxes in the car. She tore off a lid from one of the boxes and began writing the words as I sang them to her. When we arrived home, she got her accordion and began writing the notes as I sang them to her.

"Faith Can Move Mountains"

Verse one:

Faith can move mountains; faith can set men free,
Faith that moves mountains, gives me victory,
Faith is all I need today,
Since He came in to stay,
For He's broken all the bonds of sin,
And He's given peace within.

Chorus:

The Lord is all I need just now;
He's set my hands upon the plow,
He's called me to the fields today,
To help drive doubts and fears away;
He's called me to work for Him;
I know I can depend on Him,
For He's given me faith unto the end.

Verse two:

Peace flows like a river, past life's stormy sea,
Peace of God descending, Sets storm-tossed men free;
Love reigns deep within my soul,
Since Christ has made me clean,
If God now has control,
You know just what I need.

I had the song copyrighted and published in 1963. Bill Hedrick, my good friend, who was the pianist for the Sentries quartet, with whom I sang, and later, my Minister of Music at Faith Tabernacle, where I was pastor, did the arrangement.

I have watched in amazement, many miracles in my life, all orchestrated by the Holy Spirit, all brought about by faith. I pray that this book will enable you to position your life, so that you too, will experience miracle after miracle, as a result of your newfound faith. I pray that you too will see that **"FAITH CAN MOVE MOUNTAINS."**

Chapter One
THE IMPORTANCE OF FAITH

How important is faith in our lives? **Hebrews 11:6** says **"But without faith it is impossible to please him . . ."** Well, if it is impossible to please Him without faith, then I say we had better learn as much as we can about faith.

In the Bible there are many chapters that deal with great subjects. For example, in the Old Testament you have:

Isaiah 53 - The great healing chapter - verse 5, "But he was wounded for our transgressions, he was bruised for our iniquities: the chastisement of our peace was upon him; and with his stripes we are healed."

Joel 2 - The promised outpouring of the Holy Spirit/ the Baptism chapter - verses 28 and 29, "And it shall come to pass afterward, that I will pour out my spirit upon all flesh; and your sons and your daughters shall prophesy, your old men shall dream dreams, your young men shall see visions; And also upon the servants and upon the handmaidens in those days will I pour out my spirit."

Then you come into the New Testament where you have:

John 3 - The great salvation chapter - verse 16, "For God so loved the world, that he gave his only begotten Son, that whosoever believeth in him should not perish, but have everlasting life."

1 Corinthians 13 - The great love chapter - verse 1, "Though I speak with the tongues of men and of angels, and

have not charity, I am become as sounding brass, or a tinkling cymbal."

1 Corinthians 14 - The great tongues chapter - verse 2, "For he that speaketh in an unknown tongue, speaketh not unto men, but unto God; for no man understandeth him, howbeit in the spirit he speaketh mysteries."

There are other chapters, which deal with great things, but the 11th chapter of Hebrews is the **Faith chapter!** This must be one of the most important chapters in the entire Word of God. If I read it, digest it, remember it, and hide it in my heart, then maybe I will learn how to please God. According to **Hebrews 11:40, "God provided some better thing for us, that they (those heroes of faith), without us, should not be made perfect."** God, by His Word, has linked you and me, with those ancient saints of God, and has said that they are not made perfect and complete, without your faith and mine! Our faith is vitally important! Here they were—giants in faith—subduing, conquering, and enduring, and to realize, in God's eyes, we are a unit together—past, present and if Jesus tarries, that which shall be!

If God's Word says, "But without faith it is impossible to please him . . ." then the amount of faith we have will indicate the level of pleasure we bring to our God! How much pleasure are we bringing to the Lord?

Look at the godly saints back in the Old Testament. They were considered giants of faith. When God looked down and the Holy Spirit wrote about them, He said, "By faith, by faith, by faith . . ." They lived lives with which God was pleased, because He saw the faith in their lives! **Faith produces results in our lives!**

You may be fighting battles today against the enemy of your soul. You may have called upon the Lord in the past, and He may have delivered you from your fears, your sins, and your habits, but today, you may find yourself crying, "Please pray for me, and have faith for me, because I'm weak." We are to pray for one another, and to bear one another's burdens, but we are also to be responsible before the Lord and to have a faith that surpasses what our faith may have been before our previous deliverance. How permanent and how complete our deliverance is does not depend upon God! It does not depend upon God's Word! It does not depend upon a preacher or a Christian friend! **We are responsible before God for our own faith! Faith is necessary if we are going to please God!** Our faith must be consistent. There are certain things God expects from each of us.

Daniel 11:32 says " . . . **but the people that do know their God shall be strong, and do exploits.**" It is hard for people who do not know God to have faith. **1 Corinthians 2:14** says **"But the natural man receiveth not the things of the Spirit of God: for they are foolishness unto him: neither can he know them, because they are spiritually discerned."** The better you know Him, the more confidence, or faith, you have in Him. To the extent you know Him, you exercise faith, and to the extent you exercise faith, you please Him. Do you want to please Him more? Then, know Him better.

Look at God's Word, " . . . but the people that do know their God shall be **'strong.'**" The word **"strong"** here in the Hebrew means the following:

"Constant" - There will be a consistency in your life if you know God. Your life will not be like a roller coaster, up one day and down the next, if you have faith. You will not be swayed by every test or trial that comes your way, if your faith is strong. People may turn against you and may talk about you, but if you know your God, and you have faith in Him, it won't matter what they may say or do. When they see you with your head held high, and your back straight, facing every challenge the devil throws against you, they will know that it is not you, but He who lives within you, that gives you the strength and the faith to trust in Him in the midst of it all. Your life will be strong and consistent.

"Obstinate" - This means stubborn and not yielding to

reason. That is what faith does for you! It makes you strong in the Lord. I remember the story of a mother whose son was sick with a high fever. He called to his mother after he had gone to bed and said, "Mother, could you bring me an aspirin, I'm sick." She said she remembered the Scripture, **Matthew 16:18** which says " **. . . they shall lay hands on the sick and they shall recover."** She said she went upstairs and prayed for him, and the Lord healed him! She went back to bed and the devil came to her and told her, "You know, you didn't have a whole lot of faith up there a while ago." Now, that's when you need to be obstinate! She spoke out loud and said, "Satan, I had enough faith to get the job done!" There are times when we need to be "obstinate." Again, **Daniel 11:32** says " **. . . But the people that do know their God shall be strong (obstinate), and do exploits."** Faith will move mountains!

"**Wax mighty**" - This means that when the fire of the Holy Spirit begins burning in your life, even though your life may be like hardened wax, the fire will cause your life to begin melting, and you will discover a strength and might that is indescribable and beyond all earthly might. It will not be your strength, but His strength, in you. **Ephesians 6:10** says **"Finally, my brethren, be strong in the Lord, and** *in the power of his might."* **Zechariah 4:6** says " **. . . Not by might, nor by power, but by my spirit, saith the Lord of hosts."** The true source of power is not by our might, nor by our human power, but by the anointing of the Holy Spirit. This is true faith power. As our lives blend in with Him and His power, we become mighty. We get stronger and stronger as our faith in Him grows.

"**To conquer**" - The people who know God shall be conquerors (strong). Paul said in **1 Corinthians 8:35–39, "Who shall separate us from the love of Christ? Shall tribulation, or distress, or persecution, or famine, or nakedness, or peril, or sword? As it is written, For thy sake we are killed all the day long; we are accounted as sheep for the slaughter. Nay, in** *all these things* **we are** *more than conquerors* **through him** that loved us. **For I am persuaded, that neither death, nor life, nor angels, nor principalities, nor powers, nor things present, nor things to come, Nor height, nor depth, nor any other creature, shall be able to separate us from the love of God, which is in Christ Jesus our Lord."** You can see that it doesn't matter what may come our way (and the devil will see to it that many things will come our way) that if we know our God, we can trust Him to see us through because we are more than conquerors through Him. That is faith!

"Behave self" - The people who know God will behave themselves! They will not do things that will bring reproach. They will live lives that will be exemplary. Paul stated in **1 Timothy 4:12 "Let no man despise thy youth; but *be thou an example* of the believers, in word, in conversation, in charity, in spirit, in faith, in purity."** The better you know the Lord, the more faithful you will be. He will become your example. **1 Peter 1:16** says **"Because it is written, Be ye holy; for I am holy."** It is sad today to see so many, who have been good examples, falling, and losing their testimonies. They have lost their faith and have thus become weak instead of staying strong.

"Fasten upon"–The people who know God will "fasten upon Him." As their faith life lays hold, they will fasten onto the Lord and will do exploits! This reminds me of the story of the flea and the elephant: The elephant walked across a bridge with the flea riding in his ear, and when they got to the other side, the flea yelled into the elephant's ear, "Boy, didn't we shake that bridge?" **Philippians 4:13** says **"I can do all things through Christ which strengtheneth me."**

This matter of living a consistent faith life is all over the Bible—it needs to have the same emphasis in our hearts and lives that it has in God's Word!

The people who know God shall be strong (constant, obstinate, wax mighty, conquerors, behave themselves, fasten upon) and shall do exploits.

Exploits here means: "His will and pleasure." Immediately you can see that the person who knows God has confidence in Him, and that is the heart and essence of faith! The person who has faith will get a bit obstinate, and will stay that way against the enemy. That person will do **"exploits."** And, when it's all over, he or she will have accomplished God's own will and pleasure.

Chapter Two
THE EARLY DAYS

Have you ever felt there were mountains between you and where you wanted to go? You may have felt the mountains were too high to go over, or too wide to go around, and you didn't know how you were going to reach your destination.

Take a journey with me. Watch, and you will see a boy (myself) who had no faith, become someone who has seen many mountains moved. You will see how mountains of doubt and fear were moved. You will see how mountains of impossibilities were moved. The common denominator in it all was the operation of faith. Through eyes of faith I could see things becoming tangible realities. From where did that faith come?

There is a story to tell. I pray a story that will touch the hearts of people. Perhaps something that will help encourage someone else who may not have much faith at this point in his or her life. If it happened to me, it can happen to anyone.

I was born and raised in Healdton, which is a small oilfield community in South Central Oklahoma. At the time, Healdton was almost totally dependent upon "black gold." It is still true today. It was a warm, compassionate place where people loved each other. The population was about 2500. I was born in my great-grandmother's home (being born in a home was not too uncommon in those days). The date was May 28, 1937. I weighed in at ten pounds. I really didn't have such a small beginning.

I remember the small, four-room house in which I was

raised. We had a living room, a bedroom, one closet for the entire family, and a kitchen. There was a path that led to our outdoor toilet: a toilet that was cold in the wintertime and hot in the summertime. We lived next door to my grandparents, my dad's folks. Both of our families lived next to my dad's garage.

I still remember one summer day when my mother and grandmother went to the outdoor toilet at the same time. They were not small women. My grandmother McGee was just about as big around as she was tall. My mother was a large woman as well. All of a sudden, we heard blood-curdling screams, coming from the toilet and looked out to see that it had tilted over. Apparently when the two of them had sat down, their weight had caused the toilet to slide into the opening beneath it. It took my dad and grandfather quite a while to get them both out. But, thank goodness, they weren't hurt, just embarrassed.

My grandparents raised chickens. There was a chicken coup in their backyard where they were kept. Many times I would be sent to get a chicken for our dinner. We didn't go to the grocery store and get a fryer that had already been killed, cleaned, and cut up—no; we had to kill the chicken ourselves. It wasn't always the easiest thing to do. I would go into the chicken coup holding a long wire with a crook on the end. It was my job to get the fattest fryer by catching the fryer by its foot and dragging it out of the pen. Then I had to wring its neck by swinging the chicken around and around as fast as I could, and then suddenly jerking, hoping that its body would be separated from its head. I then had to clean the chicken by plucking its feathers. My mother and grandmother would then cut up the chicken so we could have delicious, homegrown, fried chicken. Now . . . those were supposed to be the good old days?

As a small boy, I would lie in front of our Christmas tree and watch the bubbling lights. We had the kind of lights that you clipped to the branches. There was liquid in the bottom of the lights, that when it became warm, would begin bubbling. They were beautiful. I thought we always had the most beautiful tree.

In my mind, I would always take exciting trips, and do exciting things, as I lay there dreaming of a house with running water and indoor toilets. I would tell my dad what I wanted for Christmas, but he would always tell me we just couldn't afford it. Then, Christmas morning would come and there would be just what I had wanted.

When I was eight, my younger brother Billy (who was six) was taken to the hospital in Duncan, Oklahoma where he had to have his enlarged spleen removed. In those days, members of the family were permitted to watch the surgery. My mother and grandmother McGee were given that privilege. They testi-fied that as they began praying, Jesus came and stood over the surgeons, with His hands outstretched, and stayed there until the surgery was over. My brother was the first one to survive that type of surgery in that hospital.

While my brother was recovering from his surgery, I developed a severe kidney infection and almost died. I remem-ber being delirious as my fever reached 105° and can still recall how it felt to see the four corners of the room coming in on me as though they were going to crush me. It all seemed so real. I'm so thankful that I had a praying mother and grandmother who knew how to get ahold of the Lord and how to pray the prayer of faith. They prayed my brother and me both through to health.

Many nights when the moon was full I would go outside and sit, sometimes for an hour at a time, and envision going to the moon. Life seemed so uncomplicated.

My mother was the one who took my brother and me to Sunday School and to church. My dad never seemed to have time to go with us. He was always too busy on Sundays. Sadly, that seems to be the case with many fathers today. They send their children to church with mom, or send them by themselves, because they're too busy, and as a result, many dads aren't lead-ing their families in spiritual things.

Throughout my childhood I had two very close friends with whom I attended church. One was my cousin, Floyd Bailey, and the other was Keith Newman, who lived across the street from me. The three of us did just about everything together. Often we would go into the woods where we would make pulpits out of tree limbs and branches. There, one of us would lead the singing, another would testify, and the other would preach. Then we would change around until we all had had the opportunity to preach. We envisioned ourselves preaching to hundreds and thousands, when in reality, there were only three of us. But, we still had wonderful services in the woods. Little did I realize that one day I would stand in front of thousands and preach the gospel! I was looking through eyes of faith into the future.

Many times my dad would take us fishing. As a child, your patience can be short, so I remember asking my dad, "Are we about there?" He would always say, "We're going to get there just before you give up." That became my philosophy in life. "I'm going to get there just before I give up!" I have reached many goals in life with that attitude as I've looked through eyes of faith.

The Lord allowed me to learn some hard lessons while growing up. I remember as boys, Keith and I would go up and down Main Street, picking up cigarette and cigar butts. We would then take all of the tobacco out (we never worried about how unclean that may have been) and smoke it in our homemade corncob pipes down by the creek close to our houses. (We certainly didn't want our parents to find us smoking.) I can still remember how sick I became smoking those corncob pipes. It wasn't long until I had dry-heaves and there wasn't anything left to come up. As a result of that experience, I could never stand to smoke. That truly became a great blessing to me in life. I can see now how the Lord kept me from developing a smoking habit.

When I was in the second grade, we moved into town. I had never seen such a house! It had five bedrooms, a living room, a dining room, a kitchen and a pantry, *and* a bathroom inside! I thought, *Boy, we have made it!* About that time we had another addition to the family. My sister Charlene was born. We were making good use of all those bedrooms.

My dad was really doing well. He owned Charlie's Garage and Body Shop, as well as the Oldsmobile, Willis Jeep, and Harley Davidson motorcycle agencies. His income in 1949 was $42,000. That was a lot of money in those days.

Then came Saturday morning, April 22, 1950. It was a beautiful morning. The sun was shining. There was not a cloud in the sky. About 6:30 A.M. the phone rang. I heard my mother as she began crying. She came into my bedroom and told me that there had been a plane crash, and that my dad was seriously injured. What was so interesting was that I was supposed to have gone with my dad and Uncle Robert that morning. They had decided not to awaken me though, because they had left earlier than they had expected to leave. The hand of the Lord was on me even then, but I did not know it.

At the time, my Uncle Robert was a flight instructor in the Air Force and he had been teaching my dad to fly. That morning my dad was to solo so he could get his pilot's license. They had taken off from the airport in Healdton where my dad kept his planes. He owned two planes at that time. They had flown to the Lake Murray airport, just south of Ardmore, Oklahoma, where my dad was practicing landing and taking off. He had just taken off, according to the man in the tower, when suddenly, the engine died. The plane nose-dived into the ground. My dad told us later that when he looked over at Robert his head was literally split open. He had died instantly.

When the man in the tower saw what had happened, he began running towards the plane. He told us that he saw my dad crawl out of the plane and begin walking. The amazing part about my dad walking was the fact he had multiple compound fractures in his legs. He had walked about twenty feet before collapsing. They pulled him away from the plane just before it burst into flames. My uncle was burned beyond recognition.

My dad was taken to an Ardmore hospital and then transferred to St. Anthony's Hospital in Oklahoma City where it was necessary to operate on both of his legs in order to repair all of the damage. After surgery his legs were put into casts and then he was put into traction. It was necessary to put pins into his ankles to hold the weights. My mom went back to our home to take care of my two younger sisters and my brother. I stayed in Oklahoma City so I could be with my dad even though I was only thirteen at the time.

My mom and dad had friends in Oklahoma City who allowed me to stay with them. They were wonderful people who attended the Nazarene church. I had the privilege of going to church with them the three months I stayed in Oklahoma City. They would take me to the hospital each morning and pick me up each evening. I'll never forget their kindness.

One morning they had taken me to the hospital and dropped me off as usual. I walked into my dad's room and saw that the traction had fallen. My dad was as white as a sheet. He was in such pain he could not utter a sound. The casts were red with blood because the weights had torn his surgery apart. I ran to the nurse's station and told them what had happened. They had to take my dad back into surgery and repair the damage that had been done. My dad then suffered a massive stroke. I do not know if it was caused by the traction falling or not. I just know that my dad's entire left side was paralyzed as a result of the stroke. After three months we were finally able to take him home.

That began two years of heartache. It became necessary to get a hospital bed so we could take care of my dad. He could not give us much help when it came to taking care of him other than to lift his right side with the help of a bar above his bed. We had to bathe him and help him go to the restroom with bedpans and urinals.

Those next two years were extremely difficult. My dad was a smart businessman in many ways, but he never felt the need for hospitalization insurance. As a result, all of the hospital bills had mounted up to an unbelievable amount. After his plane crash and hospital stay, many of the people who owed him money simply did not pay their bills. Just a small fraction, of over $26,000 that was on the books, was ever collected.

When it became very difficult to pay the hospital bills, as well as all the other bills, people in town took up money to help us. I remember years later mother showing me the list of people and the amount they had given. (That is what I was referring to earlier, when I said that the people of Healdton were compassionate and warm. They cared for and helped their own. Without their help I do not know how we would have made it.) However, after a while, that help too came to an end. It didn't take too long before we lost the business and dealerships because my dad was the one around which those revolved and, as I have stated earlier, he had no insurance of any kind.

As a result of all those things, it was not long until we were living on welfare. We received $82.00 a month from the state upon which to live. Mother had to buy groceries, pay our bills, clothe the four of us kids, and take care of all of us—that became an impossible task.

Mother began working just so we could eat and have the necessities of life. She worked in a butcher shop for minimum wage and so I had to take care of the house, do the cooking, do the housework, and take care of my younger brother and sisters. Things were not easy, but I knew there were others in the same shape.

I didn't think I would ever want pinto beans, fried potatoes, and cornbread again because it seemed like that was all we ever had to eat, but I still love them today! The Lord always supplied us food, because I don't ever remember going hungry. Sadly, there are many in the United States today, who do go to bed hungry.

I can remember mother ordering us things out of a J.C. Penney's catalog. It was always an exciting time when the mail arrived from the catalog store. We tried on the things that had once just been pictures in the book and then, knew they were ours.

When I was almost fourteen we had a revival in the small Pentecostal Holiness church where my mother would take us that would eventually change my life completely. The revival had been extended and was in its fourth week when I gave my heart to the Lord. The evangelist was Tom Manning. The Lord mightily used him. I remember he would preach an hour and a half every night!

I gave my heart to the Lord, on April 4, 1951. A few nights later I responded to the invitation to receive the baptism of the Holy Spirit. When I went forward, my brother Billy, my cousin Floyd Bailey, and one of my best friends Keith Newman and his brother Leo, all joined me in the altar. We tarried and tarried for the baptism. It seemed like we had been tarrying a long time, when in reality, it had only been a few minutes.

I remember thinking that this probably was not going to be my night to receive the Holy Spirit, so I started to get up and leave the altar area. However, to my amazement, the church people who had gathered around us to pray had hemmed in the five of us boys. There was no way out. Those people had gotten so full of the Holy Spirit in those previous three weeks, that they wanted everyone to receive what they had received.

So, I knelt back down and started praising the Lord again, and it wasn't but just a few minutes until I received the glorious infilling of the Holy Spirit, with the evidence of speaking in other tongues. It wasn't but just a few more minutes and all the rest of the boys also received the infilling of the Holy Spirit. When we received that glorious experience, the windows of heaven were opened in that little church.

I remember two sisters who began singing in the Spirit. For the next hour and a half, they sang the same language, in perfect harmony. They sounded like angels singing. People were slain under the power of God all over the church. No one was there to push them down. It was a sovereign move of the Holy Spirit.

That experience began a new work in my life. It wasn't but just a short time later that I felt the call of the Lord upon my life. I couldn't comprehend what that would mean to me at the time, I just knew the Lord wanted me to preach His Word. I couldn't understand how a person who stuttered could ever preach, but the Lord had other things in mind for me. He took care of my stuttering. He healed me!

Shortly after that experience, I was in a service where I felt the Lord in a way I don't ever remember feeling before. While in the altar praying, I began speaking in tongues, thinking in my youthful mind that I was giving a "message," but not knowing very much about the gifts of the Spirit and their operation. I truly thought I was preaching, not knowing I was out of order, because I never gave anyone an opportunity to interpret. I had gone on and on and people thought I had done a good job. Up until that point in our church we had never had any teaching on the gifts of the Spirit and their operation. So, no one knew to ask me to stop what I was doing, even though what I was doing was wrong.

I remember hearing some of the little old ladies of the church talking one night. They were talking about the five of us boys who had been saved and filled, and they said, "Those boys will never make it, serving the Lord." There was something in me that wanted to prove them wrong. I wished that I had stayed close to the Lord, but I didn't. I stumbled pretty badly throughout high school. In fact, they were right for a period of time.

During my teen years we had a pastor who dearly loved us boys. He took every opportunity to help us grow in the Lord. He let us work on the church by carrying shingles up a ladder to the men who were working. He let us haul dirt and spread it on the churchyard. He taught us the importance of taking care of God's house, even though we were just teenagers. He instilled a love in our hearts for God's house, which I still have today. God's house should always be clean and look its best.

I can look back and feel sorry for our Sunday School teachers. We boys gave them a very difficult time. I can understand now why no one wanted to teach our class. Dare I try to justify it by saying we were just growing up? I know that today, that age group, 12–14 is still a very difficult age group to reach and teach. It takes a special calling from the Lord to teach that age group.

In April of 1952, on a beautiful Sunday afternoon, a group of people from our church came to our house to see my dad. My dad had never gone to church before his accident, and after his accident, it was almost impossible to try and get him to church because of his physical condition. But, on that Sunday, he had agreed to let the people come.

They began singing and testifying and the Holy Spirit began moving on my dad. Our pastor, Fred Jones, sensing the moving of the Holy Spirit, asked my dad if he would like to give his heart to the Lord. We were thrilled when he said, "Yes!" I watched my dad cry and pray and ask the Lord to come into his heart and forgive him of all of his sins. And, I can tell you, there were many sins, according to his words. We had camp meeting in our house that day.

I still marvel at the goodness of the Lord to my dad. My dad could have lost his life the same day my uncle was killed, but my grandmother and my mother had prayed and asked the Lord to save him at any cost. It was a tremendous cost, but well worth it. Be careful when you pray, "Lord, save them at any cost."

The next Sunday my dad wanted us to take him to church. We got a wheelchair and were able to get him out of bed and took him to church for the very first time! Little did we know that the next time he would be taken to the church would be for his funeral.

I did not find out until many years later that just a couple of nights before my dad died, my cousin, Bobby Knight (who was in the Navy and was stationed in Norman, Oklahoma at the time) had come to see my dad. When Bobby went into my dad's room, my dad told him that he had had a visitor the night before. He told Bobby that the Lord had come, had stood at the foot of his bed, and had said, "Charlie, I am going to come and take you home to be with me."

When I heard about this experience, I thought, *What a wonderful, compassionate Lord!* My dad had only been a Christian a very short time, yet, the Lord loved him enough to let him know that He was coming to get him and take him home. What a wonderful Savior we serve!

I can never forget the morning of May 30, 1952, two days after my fifteenth birthday. It was about 6:30 A.M. when mother came into my bedroom, which was next to my mom and dad's. She cried, "Kenneth, don't go into my bedroom because your dad has just died." I ran into their bedroom as she ran to the phone to call for help. My dad was not dead when I arrived, but I watched him struggle for breath and tilt his head to one side and die. I will never forget that as long as I live! I loved my dad very much and still miss him to this very day.

My dad was a very strict disciplinarian. When he told you to do something, you had better do it. He wasn't like so many parents today, who will say to their children, "You are going to get it as soon as we get home." And then, they never get it! As a result, they have discipline problems. That was not so with my dad. When he said you were going to get it, you got it!

The night before my dad's funeral, I became angry with God. I couldn't stand the thought of going on without my dad, even though he had been incapacitated for two years. I left our house and started doing destructive things in town in my anger. Things became so bad that the chief of police, Bill Ratliff, arrested me and placed me in jail. The jail was dirty and stunk. It wasn't a good place to be.

Officer Ratliff let me sit in that dirty jail for quite a while, and then came in to talk to me. He told me that I had better never again do anything like I had done that night. He talked to me about my dad and told me that my dad would never have wanted me to do the things I had done that night. Then he said, "Kenneth, I'm going to let you go home so you can get some rest. I want you to be ready for your dad's funeral tomorrow." I will never forget the wisdom and kindness that Bill Ratliff showed me that night. He had lost a leg in World War I and had a wooden leg, but he had a heart as big as Texas.

The next day was very traumatic. The first time we had taken my dad to church had been just a few days before when we had taken him in a wheelchair. The next time we took him to church was when we took him in a coffin for his funeral. The church was filled to capacity for his memorial service. My dad was well-known and respected by the townspeople. Fred Jones, our pastor who had helped us in so many ways, did a wonderful job in preaching Daddy's funeral. It doesn't seem possible that my dad has been gone for fifty-one years, but he has.

When I turned sixteen, Mother surprised me with something I had wanted for years—a BB gun. I had always enjoyed hunting birds when I was younger, but had never had a good BB gun. Mother sacrificed to get me the gun, but failed to realize that I was too old for one by then. I never let on that I was too old, because I knew how hard it was for her to get me the gun.

I never had a new suit to wear, not even to our junior or senior prom. We didn't have a car, so I didn't get my driver's license until I was eighteen. My mother's brother, my uncle Clarence, wanted me to go to my senior prom, so he let me drive his new Pontiac to the prom, even though I didn't have a driver's license. I just thank the Lord that nothing happened to his car!

The last two years I was in high school, I worked at the *Healdton Herald,* our local, weekly newspaper, for ten dollars a week. I worked two hours every day after school and from eight to twelve on Saturdays. I remember George Pickle who also worked there and Little Joe, whose last name I can't remember.

During the summer I worked forty-four hours a week, still for the ten dollars a week. The money was a great blessing to us.

My senior year was exciting. I had perfect attendance in school even though I missed half the year away from classes because I was in the band, the all-school one-act play, the choir (which included the all-state select choir), the school's three act play (in which I played the lead role), and sang first tenor in the boy's quartet. The editor of the paper where I worked wrote an editorial about me receiving my perfect attendance even though I wasn't in classes but about half the time. That article caused quite a stir in town.

After graduation, the owner of the paper, John Gilder, found out that I didn't even have a suit for my graduation. He took me to a local department store and bought me my first new suit. The suit he bought me was 100% wool and came with two pair of pants. I will never forget his kindness to me. Nor will I forget how hot that wool suit was that summer. That was also the suit in which I was married, almost a year and a half later.

I did not work at the newspaper much longer after graduation. I had received a full scholarship in accounting from Midwestern University in Wichita Falls, Texas and felt I needed a better job in order to save money for things not covered by the scholarship such as food and anything extra. So, after I quit the newspaper, I got a job as a swamper (which was a helper on a truck) for A.J. Sutherland Truck Lines where I worked the rest of the summer. I earned ninety cents an hour for regular time and $1.35 an hour for overtime. Hollis Ray Allen was one of my best friends and was the driver of the truck. We had some wonderful times together hauling rigs and drill stems. One week we worked ninety hours. I had never seen so much money. My check that week was $103.50. That was quite a bit more than the ten dollars a week I had earned at the newspaper. Sadly, I became addicted to playing poker with the other men at the truck lines and began growing cold in my experience with the Lord.

I can remember coming home late at night after being

out with my friends. I would not go to bed until I had read at least one chapter from the Bible. My mother had always instilled in us kids the importance of reading the Bible every night. That was so engrained in my thinking that I could not go to bed without reading at least one chapter.

Just a little over a block away from our house was the Bethel Baptist Church. The church had chimes that played every Sunday morning. I cannot tell you how many times that summer, I would lie in bed on Sunday and listen to those chimes and feel conviction in my heart for not going to church.

Mother kept asking me to go to church. So, one Sunday evening I decided to go, just to get her off my back. I'll never forget what the Lord had in mind for the service that evening. The service had gone on as usual until the invitation was given. While the invitation was being given, I grabbed hold of the top of the pew in front of me and held so tightly, that my knuckles were turning white. I thought I had resisted the Holy Spirit's tug on my heart and had made it through another altar call without going forward.

However, the Holy Spirit kept dealing with me as I was standing there. Finally, I told the Lord if He really wanted me to serve Him, I wanted him to have the lady evangelist, Sister Mildred Wicks (who was visiting that night and who I knew did not know me) to come back and ask me to come forward. No sooner had I said that to the Lord did she raise her head from the altar, look straight at me, get up from the altar, and head right over to me. When she arrived at the pew where I was standing, she said, "Young man, wouldn't you like to come to the Lord tonight?" I couldn't resist any longer. I knew the Lord's mercy and persistence had finally won out. I returned to the same altar where just a few years before I had been saved and filled with the Holy Spirit. I renewed my dedication to the Lord and was gloriously refilled. I had simply taken a detour of a few years running away from Him.

During that time of running (my junior and senior years

of high school) I had wanted very badly to be accepted by my peers. In my desire to be accepted, I had developed terrible language. Cursing had become a big part of my vocabulary. I had become very proficient in the pool halls. In fact, very few people in town could beat me. Later, in my senior annual, I was given the title "Lord of the King's Game Table."

Even though I wasn't attending regularly, it was during those last two years of high school that I started attending the First Methodist church in town. I went because most of my friends attended there. That, too, would prove to be a blessing to me later in my life. There were many wonderful people in that church. They were very kind to me and helped me in many ways.

My grandmother McGee, whom I have mentioned earlier, was raised in the Methodist church. She had told me of the early days of Methodism, when they had brush arbor meetings, where people shouted and worshiped and praised the Lord, just as we did in the early days of the Assemblies of God. Sadly, we do not see that often in our churches today!

She told me of one brush arbor meeting that she once attended where some of the ladies asked other ladies standing close to them to hold their bobby pins. She said, "You know, you could feel a shout coming on. When you knew you were going to shout your hair down you didn't want to lose your bobby pins because they were hard to come by, so you would find ladies who were not shouters to hold your bobby pins." Today, there is no shortage of bobby pins, but where are the shouters?

After my rededication, I had a decision to make. I had gone from the height of spiritual ecstasy, to the bottom of sin, and back to the mountaintop again. I had earned a scholarship at Midwestern University in Wichita Falls, Texas. I had already reserved my room and was scheduled to enroll, but the Holy Spirit was dealing with my heart about going to Bible school and preparing for the ministry. It didn't take long for the Holy Spirit to show me what He wanted me to do. I had run long enough. It was now time to obey Him. I knew that the Lord wanted me to go to Bible school to prepare for the ministry to which He had called me.

Rev. S. N. Greene had become our pastor and was a great help in getting me accepted into Southwestern Pentecostal Holiness Bible College in Oklahoma City. The church received an offering to help me attend Bible school, and then, Brother Greene helped me get a job at Fry and House Printing Company in Oklahoma City. What I had learned by operating the presses at the Healdton Herald enabled me to work to pay my school bill. I was on my way, walking and living by faith.

Chapter Three
BIBLE SCHOOL DAYS

It was an exciting time moving to Oklahoma City to attend Southwestern Pentecostal Holiness Bible School. It was certainly different than the previous two times I had been in Oklahoma City. My dad had brought the family to Oklahoma City several years before his accident. I had never seen a place so large. Now bear in mind that the population of Healdton was 2,500 and we had a main street that was all of two blocks long. The big event on a Saturday night was to drag Main Street, that is, if you had a car. Not many of my friends had cars. As we were walking down Main Street in Oklahoma City, my dad told me I had better close my mouth, or my tonsils would get blisters from the sun. I was walking with my head tilted back and my mouth wide open, looking at all of the tall office buildings. I had never seen anything like them in my life.

The second time I came to Oklahoma City was when I was a senior in High School. I had been chosen to be in the All-State Select Choir at the University of Oklahoma in Norman, Oklahoma. Our choir director took those of us who were in the choir to Oklahoma City to eat at Jack Sussy's Italian restaurant on NE 23rd Street. I was introduced to pizza that night. I had never even heard of pizza! To my knowledge, pizza didn't exist in Healdton in 1955.

I moved onto campus in August of 1955. Dorm life was a new experience for me. That new way of life included sharing a room with five other young men, who, like myself, were all away from home for the first time in their lives. The six of us must have been real dead-heads, because we had to set two alarm clocks to awaken us.

All of the students had a responsibility to help in the kitchen. We took turns washing dishes, serving on the food line, and doing anything else that needed to be done. I was used to doing all those things, but it was a new experience for some of the kids.

Dr. R.O. Corvin, the president of Southwestern Bible College, taught my Bible class. He was a brilliant man when it came to the knowledge of God's Word. If anyone in the class challenged our answer to a question, he would have us stand and defend our answer. His Bible class taught me the importance of *knowing* the Word of God, just as my mother had taught me the importance of *reading* the Word. I still have some of his Bible study courses.

Brother Corvin was also a man of prayer. He taught us, through his example, the importance of prayer. He told us how God miraculously supplied the needs for the Bible school and in his own personal life. The things he instilled in our lives became so important in my life later. He taught us we could depend on the Lord to supply our needs. He taught us that the Lord never fails. He taught us the importance of the moving of the Spirit in our lives and in our worship services.

Many times in our chapel services, the Holy Spirit would simply take over, and the school officials would cancel the class scheduled for the next hour. Our chapel services would turn into prayer meetings and worship. I praise the Lord for the leaders we had in school, who allowed the Holy Spirit to move and operate; thus letting us know that the important thing in our services is the moving of the Holy Spirit.

One morning, as we gathered for chapel service, they brought one of the students who had fallen and broken his leg, into the chapel. (He had asked to be brought to chapel before he was taken to the hospital.) You could see that he was in excruciating pain as Dr. Corvin, Dr. Harold Brooks, (the dean of men), and several of the teachers and professors gathered around him to pray. As we were praying, the Holy Spirit spoke to my heart, "Go, lay your hands on him and pray." I wrestled with the Lord and said, "But Lord, I am no one. I'm just a freshman and those are all great men of God who are praying for him." The Holy Spirit kept speaking, "Go, lay your hands on him and pray!" I stood there until I thought my heart would jump out of my body because it was pounding so hard. I began crying and finally said, "Lord, if you want me to go and lay my hands on him and pray, I will."

I walked up the aisle to where they were praying for him, reached over, laid my hands on him, and asked the Lord to heal him. Instantly, the Lord healed him! The Lord was teaching me the importance of being obedient to Him. He was teaching me that if I would be sensitive to Him, He could use me. My faith was growing. The truth is He can use any yielded vessel that will become a channel through which He can flow. You simply have to be hungry to be used by Him!

Southwestern had what I thought was an unusual rule for the school. It was called the no-touch rule. You were not permitted to hold hands with the opposite sex nor were you permitted to kiss. As you might imagine, that rule was broken often. If you were caught breaking the rule, you were brought before the student council. The punishment? You could not leave the campus and you had to do extra kitchen duty. There were a number of times in our chapel services when the Holy Spirit was moving that young people would get up and confess that they had broken the no-touch rule. Those were special times, because no one laughed and thought it was funny when the confessions were made. The Holy Spirit simply brought conviction to those who had broken the rule.

Now don't think that there wasn't any dating going on because of the rule because there was a lot of dating. If you wanted to go out on a date you simply had to find a chaperon for your date. The chaperon was to assure that the no-touch rule was not broken. It was the chaperon's responsibility to let the school officials know what happened on the date. To get around the rule you would simply find someone to be your chaperon who could "see no evil, hear no evil or speak no evil!" Where there's a will, there's a way!

I had not been at the school very long when the Lord began dealing with me about something that had happened back in Healdton. I would get down to pray and the same thing kept coming back, again and again. I had had a good friend in Healdton, with whom I had attended school, whose dad owned the Mobil gas station in town. One day as I was going home after school I had stopped at the service station and got a coke, which then cost a nickel. I did not pay for the coke when I left. However, the next day, after my conscience began bothering me, I stopped by and told the owner that I had forgotten to pay for a coke the day before, and gave him a nickel for the coke.

I had left town and gone to Bible school and forgotten about what I had done, after all, it was just a nickel coke. But, the Holy Spirit had not forgotten. I knew that I was in school, preparing for the ministry, and the Holy Spirit had brought that experience back to mind. How could I stand and preach the gospel when I had stolen and lied about that coke? I knew that I must go back home, and go to the man, and tell him what I had done if I wanted peace in my heart. I went back home and walked into the service station and found the owner. I told him that I was in Bible school, preparing for the ministry, but that there was something that I had to tell him. I told him what I had done, that I had stolen the coke, and then came back the next day and lied to him, telling him that I had forgotten to pay him, but, that I had given him the nickel for the coke. I told him I wanted to give him a dime and asked him to forgive me. He wouldn't take the dime, but he told me what it had meant to him to have me come back and tell him what I had done. There were tears in his eyes when he told me. I know one thing, when I left, I felt as though a ton had rolled off of me. I had peace in my heart, knowing I had done what the Lord wanted me to do. After that it was a lot easier to go back to school and to do my studies.

I'm afraid that there are many times in our lives when the Holy Spirit may speak to our hearts to do something, that we may feel "isn't that big of a deal," and because we don't respond to His urging, we miss the blessing He has in store for us. I know that I have shared my experience involving the nickel coke many times in my ministry, and that I would not have had that experience to share had I not been obedient to the Lord. It proved to be another rung on my ladder of faith.

In 1955, I had the privilege of playing on the school's first basketball team. We didn't have many players and we may not have been very good, but we sure had a great time. One of the teams we played was Bethany Nazarene College. Today it is known as Southern Nazarene University, a wonderful school that excels in sports as well as academics. We had a game scheduled with them during the Christmas vacation. The game was played at the First Baptist Church gym, which was located at 11th and Robinson in Oklahoma City. We only had five players from Southwestern for the game, because two or three had gone home for Christmas, while Bethany had twelve players. They simply ran us ragged. The final score was over 100 to maybe 20.

I joined the choir and also played my trombone in the orchestra. Sybil Grisham was our choir director. She took such an interest in all of us students, and allowed us to grow in the Lord. She taught us the importance of knowing the music, and the importance of allowing the Holy Spirit to move among us. Paul told us in **2 Corinthians 3:6, " . . . the letter killeth, but the spirit giveth life."** I can still remember some of the wonderful services when the Holy Spirit would take over and all heaven would come down.

We were in one church where the choir loft had an opening going down into the basement. I could never understand why they would have left an opening where you could fall into the basement, but they had. The choir began singing and the Holy Spirit began moving. It wasn't long until several of the choir members began dancing in the Spirit. I watched, as they would dance over close to the opening to the basement, and yet never fall into the basement. As the Spirit moved in the choir, He moved among the congregation. The glory of the Lord filled the church that night. We had messages in tongues and interpretation of tongues in our choir services. People were saved, filled with the Holy Spirit, and healed in our services.

I was still on campus when Christmastime arrived that first year. Something happened at that time which would change my life forever. I was in the girl's dorm (which was supposed to be off limits to us boys) when a young lady by the name of Gretnia Grant came to invite some of the girls to her Christmas party. I remember thinking how pretty she was. I just didn't know then what the Lord's plan was for our lives. I was to find out later that she was the one who the Lord had chosen to be my helpmate for life.

It was not long after the first of the year in 1956 that I received word that my brother Billy was hemorrhaging badly and was being brought to Oklahoma City. I met my mother at University Hospital where they had taken him. During one 24-hour period, it was necessary to give him 32 pints of blood. The blood bank at the hospital got so low on A+ blood, which is what they were giving Billy, that it became necessary to take blood from my mother and me and infuse it directly into Billy. Things have changed dramatically since that period of time in how hospitals handle blood. Today, there are many more requirements necessary before blood is given to an individual.

Billy's condition became so critical that people from Healdton, our hometown, came in caravans to give blood for him. It was a sight I will never forget, seeing one carload of people after another, coming to University Hospital, to give blood for my brother. I remember being in study hall one night when

I received word from the hospital that if I wanted to see Billy alive I needed to get to the hospital as quickly as possible. Harold Brooks, our dean of men, took me to the hospital.

When I left the study hall, the entire student body began a prayer meeting that lasted for almost two hours. Praise the Lord for a school body, and leaders of that school, who knew the importance of prayer. When I arrived at the hospital, the doctors met with my mother and me and told us that they had been able to stop the bleeding, but that if Billy began bleeding again, they didn't know what else they could do. As they were explaining the situation to us, the nurses came running out of Billy's room and told the doctors that Billy was bleeding again.

As mother and I were standing there with the doctors, they began talking to each other about trying something that had just come to their minds. They decided to insert two tubular balloons through Billy's nose to reach the area that was bleeding and to inflate the balloons with enough pressure to stop the bleeding. They felt that if that would work, it would allow the blood to coagulate, thus giving them enough time to operate. And, praise the Lord, it worked! In fact, that became a standard medical practice for that type of problem. All of this came about, I believe, because the student body of Southwestern was praying. Prayer changes things and people.

The surgery took eleven-and-a-half hours. That was a long time to be under anesthesia. A team of surgeons alternated times during the day as they worked to save Billy's life. The Lord had His hand over Billy, just as He had done when Billy had his spleen removed. The doctors were amazed that Billy had made it through the surgery—it was a miracle because Billy had been in such a weakened condition when the surgery began.

Sybil Grisham asked Billy to accompany the choir when the choir took its spring concert tour. He shared his testimony in all of our church services. It was a tremendous miracle that blessed the hearts of many people. You may wonder, *how could that be considered a miracle, when it took the doctors to save his life?* Well, it was a miracle because the doctors were inspired to begin a procedure that would save the lives of many people. That procedure, I believe, was in answer to the prayers of many students who sought the face of the Lord the night that Billy was so critically ill.

While at Southwestern we were required to attend Muse Memorial Pentecostal Holiness church, which was directly across from where the school was located. Many times, however, a group of us would attend Faith Tabernacle, which was located at 1110 N.W. 2nd Street. I was attending Faith Tabernacle on April 1, 1956, when Bobby and Loretta Greene asked me if I would like to invite Loretta's sister, Gretnia Grant, the beautiful young lady I had met during the Christmas holidays in the girl's dorm at Southwestern, to go with me to Cattlemen's Steak House. They told me that we could all go together if she said yes to my invitation. After she told me she would go with me, the four of us were invited to ride to the restaurant with Ronnie VanHorn and his date, Carol, in his white Cadillac convertible. That night changed the rest of my life! I found out later that Loretta had told Gretnia that if I ever asked her to go out with me that she had better not refuse. I'm glad Loretta told her that. I'm also glad that she helped arrange the first date for me. Gretnia and I began dating after that Sunday night.

I had to drop out of school at that point, due to the fact that I had missed so many classes helping Billy get out of the hospital and back on his feet that I didn't have time to catch up on my studies before the school year ended. I started working at Weber's drive-in root beer stand, at 12th and North Pennsylvania in Oklahoma City, which was owned by Bobby Greene and Tommy Grant, Gretnia's dad.

I was working one Sunday afternoon at the root beer stand when Billy Graham's crusade service ended at the state fair arena. Within a few minutes the entire lot was filled. I had three carhops working with me that day which would normally have been sufficient to handle the crowd, but not that day. The carhops would call out the orders, and I would repeat the orders, and then fill them so they could take the orders out. There were so many people that afternoon that I used all of the frosted mugs that I had available. I then had to wash the mugs before I could reuse them. I had to prepare all of the hot dogs, ham sandwiches, root beer floats, and root beer whips, (which were made by blending root beer and ice cream), as well as fill the mugs. I did more in sales in a two-hour period that day than the root beer stand had ever done in an entire day. Just as the business was slowing down, Bobby and Tommy drove up to see the entire counter filled with empty mugs. The two of them had gone to Dallas to pick up supplies without realizing the Billy Graham crusade was in town and that I had no one else to help me. That was an experience I will never forget.

One day while working at the root beer stand, Donnie Moody, a young man who attended First Assembly of God, stopped by to order a root beer. I began talking to him and discovered that he had drifted away from the Lord. The Holy Spirit gave me an opportunity to witness to him and to ask him if he would like to give his heart back to the Lord. It was wonderful to see him pray through and surrender to the Lord. Within the next few days the young man and his family left to go to California for their vacation. While driving on one of the freeways in California, a truck crossed over the median and struck their car head-on. Donnie was killed instantly. The Lord had given him a chance to give his heart back to Him and, praise the Lord, he had.

My experiences at Southwestern were a great blessing to me. The Lord kept me on an exciting journey. He helped prepare me for a ministry that was coming in the near future. He taught me the importance of studying His word. He gave me friends and relationships that would follow me the rest of my life. He taught me the importance of being yielded to the Holy Spirit. He taught me not to be afraid to trust Him. He showed me that He was a prayer-answering God. He showed me that if I would be obedient to Him, He would perform miracles. He brought a beautiful young lady into my life.

I was ready for another chapter in my life. My faith was growing. I was learning to trust Him more.

Chapter Four
GETTING READY FOR MINISTRY

1956 proved to be an exciting year. I witnessed miracles, was taught God's Word, experienced Bible School, and found the girl of my dreams. What more could I want? I began attending Faith Tabernacle after the school year was over because that is where Bobby and Loretta Greene were attending, and, that is where Gretnia was attending. The church started a men's fast-pitch softball team that summer. I had the privilege of playing left field on the team. We usually played two games a week and that provided a good time for Gretnia and me to be together. I knew all the time I was going to Bible school that the Lord had called me to preach, and I was diligently seeking the Lord about who He wanted me to marry. I felt in my heart that Gretnia was the person He had chosen for me. I prayed that she would feel the same way about me.

In June of 1956, two months after we had our first date, I asked Gretnia to marry me. I was thrilled when she said yes, and I gave her an engagement ring. I must admit that I was surprised that her mom and dad agreed to let us get married because she was only fifteen at the time and I had just turned nineteen. Both of them, however, seemed to like me, even though, Tommy, Gretnia's dad, told her he would buy her a new organ if she didn't marry me. He had already bought her a beautiful, new, gray and white 1956 Chevrolet Impala two-door hardtop, with a continental kit on the back. It was a beautiful car. I wish we still had it today!

That summer was a wonderful time as Gretnia and I enjoyed being together in all of the activities of the church. I took her to Healdton to meet my mother, sisters, and brother. They all fell in love with her as well. As the months passed by we began to argue with each other and finally the night came when she gave me back her engagement ring. I was devastated! I took the ring and gave it to Bobby and Loretta Greene for them to keep. I told Gretnia that if she ever wanted it back she knew where to find it.

I had already decided not to return to Southwestern Bible School for the fall semester, but I wasn't sure about what I was going to do. While I was praying about the Lord's will for my life, I received a phone call from Bobby Jenkins, a good friend I had met at Southwestern. Bobby was one of the best preachers I had ever heard. There was a special anointing on his ministry. He was in revival in Springfield, Colorado, at the time and he told me that he had talked to the pastor about seeing if I could come and help him in the revival. He wanted me to lead the worship and sing special music. He told me if I would come that he and the pastor would drive to Oklahoma City after their evening service, pick me up, and take me back to be with them the next night. I couldn't imagine that he would want me to come and help in his revival. However, there was something that clicked in my heart when he asked me and so I told him I would be ready the next morning. I quickly packed my clothes and was ready when they arrived the next morning. I was leaving Gretnia, but I had to put the situation in the Lord's hands. It was a difficult thing to do but I knew that if it were God's will for us to be together, and she was the one He had chosen for me, then He would work it all out.

I led the worship the first night there and sang special songs and then turned the pulpit to Bobby to preach. I wasn't prepared for his announcement. He announced that I would be preaching the Sunday morning message! The date was Thursday night, October 11, 1956. I didn't know what to think. I knew the Lord had called me to preach, but I didn't know it would be so soon. Bobby told me he would help me prepare the message for Sunday morning. I had taken the courses and done the training in Bible school, but suddenly I would be preaching for real!

The next two days were spent preparing the message and preparing my heart. (Both are equally important.) **2 Corinthians 3:6** states, **" . . . the letter killeth, but the spirit giveth life."** I knew that you could have all the points and be homiletically right, but if the anointing was not there, your words would be as Paul said in **1 Corinthians 13:1, " . . . as sounding brass, or a tinkling cymbal."**

My first message was entitled, "The Nightingale of the Psalms." Bobby had a booklet by that name, and when he asked if I would like that subject, I told him I would. I do not know the author of that booklet, nor do I know if there were other subjects in the booklet, because there was no cover on it. I do still have the pages in my possession today though, as well as the first message I preached. I am indebted to whoever wrote that booklet.

As I prepared the outline to my message, I began bathing it in prayer. I knew that I couldn't stand before the congregation on Sunday morning and preach God's Word without His anointing. Back in those days the revivals went seven days a week. So, after the Saturday evening service I went back to the church and began praying for the service the next morning. I stayed at the church and prayed until almost four o'clock Sunday morning. I then got up at 6:00 A.M. and began praying again.

I'll never forget standing behind the pulpit that Sunday morning, October 14, 1956, at the Pentecostal Holiness church in Springfield, Colorado. I never had to wait for a word or a thought. I had great liberty as the words flowed for twenty-five minutes. When I gave the invitation, four people came forward to give their hearts to the Lord. Whatever ministry the Lord was giving to me had just begun. The faith to trust and believe in Him was growing. I'll never forget the presence of the Lord I felt that morning!

A wedding was scheduled to take place at the church before the revival service on Tuesday, October 16th. Albert Maggard and Mary Harbert, two young people who had attended Southwestern with me and Bobby, were getting married. (The church in Springfield was Mary's home church.) Although the ceremony was supposed to occur *before* the revival service, Albert and Mary had still not arrived by the time the service was scheduled to start and so we went on with the service; in fact, they still had not arrived by the time the service was over. They finally arrived about 10:00 P.M. Mary went in to change into her wedding gown while Bobby was playing the piano. He then started playing the wedding march, but had to play it over and over again while she was getting ready. I was seated next to Bobby on the piano bench so I could turn the pages of music for him.

The pastor of the church began the wedding ceremony when Albert and Mary were finally ready. When the pastor told Albert he could kiss his bride, Albert turned Mary around and tilted her back as he kissed her. When he turned to kiss her, he was facing Bobby and me. Albert had to wear thick glasses because of his vision problem. Well, Albert never closed his eyes when he kissed Mary. In fact, it looked as though his eyes were greatly enlarged when he kissed her, because of the amplification of his glasses. Bobby and I became so tickled we could hardly sit there. Mary did not know that Albert had not closed his eyes until I called them to see if I had their permission to tell their story.

Bobby and I closed the revival in Springfield and drove to Palisade, Colorado, for our next revival. We had to drive over Loveland pass to get to Palisade. As is typically the case at that time of the year, it was snowing like crazy, and as a result we were almost late getting to the church. When we arrived, we went down into the basement of the church to change clothes. While we were changing we began hearing some strange sounds. We opened the door and saw two ladies, who happened to be sisters, each with a broom, sweeping the basement and waving their brooms into the air. We asked what they were doing, and they informed us they were sweeping all of the devils out of the church so that we could have a revival. Bobby and I looked at each other and wondered what all was going to happen in the revival. It didn't take us long to find out.

Just a couple of nights later, some children who were sitting on the front row became unruly while Bobby was preaching. He stopped in his message and asked the parents to come and get their children because they were disturbing the service. The father, who was seated on the back row, got up, came forward, jerked his children up by the hands, and said loudly, "Come on and let's get out of here. And, I tell you, we won't be back!" With those words, they walked out of the church. Boy did the church get quiet. Bobby asked the congregation to pray for the man and his children and continued his message. When he gave the invitation, people came forward to give their hearts to the Lord. Two nights later, the man returned, with his children, and when the invitation was given, he and his children came forward and gave their hearts to the Lord. He then stood and apologized for what he had done and for the way he had allowed his children to act in church. I am amazed at how many parents today will let their children sit at the front of the church, unsupervised, while they sit in the back of the congregation. As a result, many problems are caused because the children have no supervision.

We were having a lot of visitors coming to the meeting. I don't know if having two, young, unmarried evangelists had anything to do with it or not, but people were coming, especially young ladies. The two sisters I had mentioned earlier, who had been sweeping the devils out of the basement when we first arrived, always sat on the front row. One of them was very demonstrative, letting out some very strange sounds during the services. She had her hair done up into a bun on the back of her head. One night a beautiful young lady came to visit and sat on the back row. As the service progressed, the sister who made the strange sounds suddenly got to her feet and began making a sound like, "Ooh, ooh, ooh," in a high pitched voice. She began dancing across the front of the church, then danced down the aisle, making her way to the back of the church, where she went and stood behind the young lady who was visiting. Suddenly she grabbed the young lady's head with her hands, and began shaking her violently. It nearly scared the young lady to death. Praise the Lord, the girl did not get up and run out of the church. She stayed until the service was over. Interestingly, no one said anything to the sister who had shaken the girl's head.

In Springfield, Bobby and I had stayed with the pastor and his wife in the church parsonage. When we arrived in Palisade, the pastor there placed us with a family that had a two-story house. We had the loft on the second floor. The people were very nice, but they had several children. It wasn't the quietest place in the world, but the food was great. I still remember the delicious Alberta peaches, for which Palisade was famous, that they served at meal times.

We had not been in the church but a few nights when Bobby announced that I would be preaching the first Sunday morning service of the revival. I was thrilled that I was getting to preach again. However, I learned a very important lesson at that time. I remembered how easy it had been to preach the first time in Springfield. As a result of it being so easy, I didn't stay up until four o'clock Sunday morning praying as I had done in Springfield. I was going to preach the same sermon, so I thought I would remember all of the thoughts I had had the first time I preached and therefore I did not spend the time in prayer as I had done the first time.

That Sunday morning Bobby introduced me and turned the service over to me for the message. I'll never forget the second time I preached, just as I'll never forget the first time I preached. I felt as though I was spitting cotton for the next ten minutes. I searched for words and thoughts that never came. I don't know when I have ever been as miserable in the pulpit as I was that morning. I gave the invitation and nothing happened. I was devastated. The Lord let me fall flat on my face, so that I would learn to diligently seek and depend upon Him. I discovered quickly that it's " . . . **not by might, nor by power, but by my spirit, saith the Lord of host" (Zechariah 4:6).** I have never forgotten what happened to me that morning. I didn't have the ability or the knowledge to preach without His divine help.

The pastor came to me one day during the second week we were there and asked if anything was wrong. Evidently, I had been acting as though I were unhappy. He thought that perhaps I needed to call and talk to my mom. He took me to the parsonage and let me call her that day. It was good to talk to Mother. She informed me that I had received a notice from the draft board telling me that I would not be drafted. I knew then that I wouldn't have to go to boot camp. That was good news because I had worried about what would happen if Gretnia and I got back together and we decided to get married.

Although it was nice to talk to my mother, I wasn't really missing her all that much—I was missing Gretnia! I was wondering what she was doing and how she was making it since I had been gone. I wondered if she were missing me like I was missing her. I was praying diligently every day for the Lord's will to be done in our lives. If He wanted Gretnia to be my wife and helpmate in whatever ministry He had for me, then He would have to put our lives back together.

By this time, I had been gone more than a month. Revivals always lasted at least two weeks in those days and this was our second revival. We had wonderful services during the rest of the revival. A number of people were saved and filled with the Holy Spirit. There were some outstanding miracles of healing. I watched the Lord answer many prayers. My faith was growing. I was learning to depend more and more on Him. I discovered

He was faithful, and that I could depend on Him to supply all my needs.

We closed that revival and drove back to Oklahoma City where our next meeting was scheduled. It seemed to take forever to get to Oklahoma City. I was anxious to see if Gretnia wanted to see me when I got back. The night we got into town, Bobby Jenkins took me to Bobby and Loretta Greene's house where I was going to stay during the revival we had scheduled at the First Pentecostal Holiness church. I called Gretnia the next day to see if she would see me that night. She came to Bobby and Loretta's house that evening. We began talking and sharing with each other how much we had missed each other. She had not been there very long when we went into the kitchen. (That is where I had left her ring.) She went over to where the ring had been kept, took it out, and put it back on her finger. The Lord had been working in her heart while I was gone, just as He had been working in my heart. It seemed as though we had never been apart. We decided to get married on December 29th.

Bobby Jenkins and I held the revival at the church. I can tell you, I was sure a lot happier at that revival than I had been in the previous revival. Scott and Ina Taylor attended the church where we were preaching the revival. Scott had been in the Gospel Stars quartet that had come to Healdton, my hometown. Ina played the organ during the revival. They were to become lifelong friends to Gretnia and me. Scott gave me a beautiful orchard-colored sport coat during the revival. I wore that sport coat for a long time.

Things began moving very quickly as we began planning our wedding. Gretnia had told me that her two brother-in-laws, Bill Mash and Bobby Greene, had to ask her dad if they could marry her two sisters, Laquitta and Loretta. She told me that her dad was expecting me to ask him for her hand in marriage as well.

Jack and Gladys Felkins, close friends of Gretnia's mom and dad, had our wedding shower at their house. There was a wonderful turnout as many from the church came. We received a lot of wonderful gifts. Wedding showers are a great blessing to young people.

Charles Horsley, a close family friend and comic, brought an ink pen to the shower that was supposed to have disappearing ink. He walked up to Russell E. Pratt, the minister of music at Faith Tabernacle, who happened to be wearing a white suit, opened his ink pen, and squirted Brother Pratt's suit. Everyone gasped when they saw what had happened. Brother Pratt's beautiful white suit suddenly had black ink all over it. Charles told Brother Pratt, and everyone else, that the ink would disappear in a few minutes. We all waited and waited, but the stain never disappeared. They had to take the suit to the cleaners to get the stain out.

Our wedding was scheduled for Saturday, December 29th, but when Friday, December 28th came (the day we were to go to the courthouse to get our license) I still had not asked Gretnia's dad for her hand in marriage. Her dad and I went to the courthouse to get the marriage license. (It was necessary for him to sign for the license because Gretnia was only sixteen.) It wasn't until we stepped off of the elevator in the courthouse that I finally turned to him and asked him if I could marry his daughter. His face turned red, but he said "Yes!" Praise the Lord! He told me later that he would have given anything if he had just thought and said "No," just to see what I would have done. I know one thing, I'm sure glad he didn't.

Gretnia and I had decided not to have a big church wedding. We just wanted to get married in Pastor S. J. Scott's office. Brother Scott was the pastor of Faith Tabernacle which was the largest Assembly of God church in Oklahoma City at that time. It was number one in missions giving in the state of Oklahoma. It had an outstanding choir and orchestra. And it was known all over the state for it's beautiful Christmas and Easter dramas, all directed by Leanetta Scott, Brother Scott's wife.

Saturday, December the 29th, finally arrived. I wore the

suit to be married in that I had been given when I worked at the Healdton Herald. That suit had been a real blessing to me. We all gathered at Faith Tabernacle for the service—Gretnia and I, her mother and dad, Thomas H. and Gurtha Grant, my mother, Juanita McGee, my aunt, Stella Knight, and Rev. and Mrs. S. J. Scott. We were all in Brother Scott's office for our ceremony. I believe I know how Belshazzar must have felt, because my knees smote one against the other as we stood there going through the ceremony. I don't believe I could have handled a big church wedding. If I became that nervous with just a few people, I would probably have passed out with a larger crowd.

After the ceremony at the church we all went to Gretnia's home where her mother had prepared a beautiful reception for our family members and close friends. After the reception Gretnia and I were taken to downtown Oklahoma City where a wheelbarrow was waiting for us. I put Gretnia into the wheelbarrow and started wheeling her down Main Street. After I had rolled her a block, I was put into the wheelbarrow and she rolled me a block. After we had each rolled each other a block, we were given a roll of toilet paper. We then had to stop people on the street and sell them a sheet of toilet paper for a penny apiece so we could buy bubble gum for everyone. I thought that was the end of what they had planned for us, but I found out quickly that there were even more things they had in mind.

After we left downtown Oklahoma City, we were taken to a friend's apartment on N.W. 10th Street where I was given a chance to change clothes. I was told I needed to change clothes if I were going swimming. Now bear in mind this was December 29th, in the middle of winter, and it was cold! We were taken to a home across the street from Southwestern Bible College where I had attended school, where a swimming pool was waiting. The pool was full of water and the cover had been removed. I was given a choice of either jumping in or being thrown in. I thought if I was going swimming, I had rather do it on my terms, so I jumped into the pool.

While I was getting out of the pool, some of Gretnia's girlfriends took her and kept her away from me for quite some time. Not only was I upset, but my mother and aunt were very upset as well. Everyone else thought that the whole thing was funny. There was nothing else to do but to go back to Gretnia's house and wait for the girls to bring Gretnia back. It was almost two hours before they brought her back. It turned out that they had just been driving around town the whole time.

At last we were able to go to our apartment on N.W. 9th. We were married! A new chapter in our lives was beginning.

Chapter Five
SINGING AND PREACHING

Our first year of marriage proved to be quite eventful. Gretnia was attending high school at Southwestern Bible School and I was working downtown at a department store. We were getting more and more involved at Faith Tabernacle where I became the president of Christ Ambassadors, the youth group of the church. Taking Gretnia to school, going to work, and going back to pick her up, meant quite a lot of driving every day. We got home from church one Sunday evening and noticed that the gas gauge was on empty. I would not get paid until the following Friday and we didn't have enough money for gasoline for the week. There was nothing else to do about our situation except pray. We did not call our families to ask for help, but we did get down and asked the Lord to provide enough gasoline until I got paid Friday. We didn't know any better than to trust the Lord. After all, hadn't he said in His Word, **"But my God shall supply all your need according to his riches in glory by Christ Jesus" (Philippians 4:19).**

We went out the next morning to start the car and when I turned the ignition on, the gas gauge went up to over half-full. That was more than enough gasoline to last us the week. We knew the Lord had performed a miracle for us. The Lord was teaching us that we could depend on Him, and that He would supply our every need. He is **"Jesus Christ the same yesterday, and today, and forever" (Hebrews 13:8).** Our faith was growing!

Being C.A. president gave me an opportunity to preach each week. I began taking our youth to different nursing homes in the area for Sunday afternoon services. It proved to be a great blessing for our youth as they were able to minister to the older people. We had service one Sunday afternoon in a nursing home, which was located just West of May Avenue. After our worship service I gave an invitation. We had some respond to the invitation for which we were thankful. It had been a wonderful service. However, as we were leaving, I passed by the bed of an elderly gentleman who had been unable to come to the service. He stopped me and told me he would like to give his heart to the Lord, and asked if I would pray for him. I told him I would be thrilled to pray for him, but before I could pray, several members of his family came to visit, and I was unable to lead him to the Lord. He asked if I could come back the following week and pray with him. I assured him that I would. I don't remember what happened, but I did not get by to pray for him until the following Sunday. When I went to his room, he was not there. I asked where he was and the staff informed me that he had died that week.

I have never forgotten that experience. It still haunts me today. I just pray that he remembered what I had been saying to the others and that he had called upon the Lord. We need to always take advantage of the opportunities we have at the moment, because we may never have the same opportunity later. It was D.L. Moody who said, "To recall the following act I would give my right hand. On the night when the Court House bell of Chicago was sounding an alarm of fire, my sermon was upon 'What Shall I Do With Jesus?' And I said to the audience, 'I want you to decide this question by next Sunday.' What a mistake! That night I saw the glare of the flames, and knew that Chicago was doomed. I never saw that audience again."

Brother Scott was always good to let young ministers fill his pulpit on different occasions. He told two other young ministers and me that we would have the pulpit one Sunday night.

He would give each of us ten minutes in the service. The night finally arrived. I had prayed about what I would preach because I had already exhausted my entire repertoire of sermons. I didn't have that many sermons to begin with and I had already preached them in our youth services. I will never forget the message the Lord gave me for that Sunday night because I still have the original copy.

"Now Is The Hour"
John 5:24–29

Introduction: Man at Bethesda - healed body and soul.

1. Everyone is having the chance to hear the Word of life.
    a. Radio   **c. Missionary**
    b. TV   **d. Evangelist**

One person dies every 30 seconds in the United States. That is 2880 every day. 120 people in the world die every minute. That is 172,800 a day. How many know the Lord?

2. No man cometh to me except by the Father.
    a. You can't get saved just anytime you want to get saved.
    b. You must be drawn by the Holy Spirit.
    c. Pearl Harbor, December 7, 1941—things would have been done differently had they known what was going to happen.
    d. Ephesians 2:1–5

3. You are at the pathway of your spiritual life.
    a. John 5:25 "Verily, verily, I say unto you, The hour is coming, and now is, when the dead shall hear the voice of the Son of God: and they that hear shall live."

b. What will it be—Heaven or Hell?

4. "It is appointed unto man once to die, after that, the judgment."
    a. Death is sure.
    b. You will stand before the judgment bar.

5. Be ready to meet the Lord!
    a. Matthew 24:36–51
    b. 1 Thessalonians 4:16–17
    c. 1 Corinthians 15:50–52

Conclusion: Tell about Donnie Moody.

When I got up to preach that night I must admit I was really nervous. As I was preaching, I came to a place where I said, **"Pert near."** I don't ever remember saying that before, but I did that night. Faith Tabernacle, as I have said before, was a large downtown church, with a number of professional people in the congregation. When I made that statement, everyone began to laugh. I just about lost it. However, the Lord was good to me and helped me finish the message. We had a wonderful service that night in spite of my **"Pert near."**

Our son, Kenny, was born on November 23, 1957. The doctor had told us all during Gretnia's pregnancy that we were going to have a girl. I kept telling Gretnia that we were going to have a boy. Those were the days before ultrasound so we didn't know ahead of time what we were going to have.

I was working at Lefevre Chemical Company that Saturday morning, November 23rd, earning time and a half, when Gretnia called and told me that she thought her water had broken and that she was going to the hospital. I left work, drove quickly home, and ran into the duplex where we were living, only to find that Gretnia was not there. I was beside myself, not knowing what had happened, when the phone rang. It was Gretnia, calling from her mother's house, to tell me she was all right. (She had gone to her mother's house to take a shower before she went to the hospital because we didn't have a shower in our duplex.)

Laquitta, Gretnia's sister, had gone to the hospital earlier that morning and had given birth to a beautiful baby girl, Brenda Sue. Gurtha Grant, Gretnia's mother, thought that perhaps all the excitement of Laquitta having her baby had caused Gretnia to go into labor, because it was still three weeks before she was due. We arrived at the hospital and they placed Gretnia in the labor room. Gretnia's mother and I were asked to stay with her and to keep her still, so she wouldn't sit up.

Finally they came and took Gretnia into the delivery room. We waited and waited and finally Dr. Jim Eskridge came out and told us we had a baby **"boy!"** I could hardly believe my ears, we had a boy. As soon as they brought Gretnia out, I told her, "We have a boy!" Needless to say, we were excited. We are still excited and proud of our boy!

Since Laquitta had given birth to Brenda that morning and Gretnia had given birth to Kenny that night, the hospital put them together in the same hospital room. Their picture was on the front page of the Daily Oklahoman. It was highly unusual for sisters to be in the same room, having given birth to babies on the same day.

In the fall of 1958 I was asked to sing with the group that had formally been known as the "Gospel Stars." Bill Hedrick had been away in the Army and when he returned we started a new group. We decided to call ourselves the "Sentries." We felt we were sentries for the Lord in His work. The group consisted of Scott Taylor, Bobby Greene, Ken Black, Bill Hedrick and me. We traveled and sang together until 1961. During that period of time the Lord opened many doors for us. We sang at the "Rainbow Singings" in the Municipal Auditorium, downtown Oklahoma City, with the Sooner State Boys on numerous occasions. In fact, we recorded a long play record with them entitled, "A Day at the Rainbow Singing." The "Rainbow Singings" began the second Sunday of September 1936. They had become an important spiritual and inspirational must to the community. They were usually held on the second Sunday of each month. It was always a great joy to sing there.

We sang with Tony Fontaine in the Civic Center Music Hall before over 7500 people. We also sang with the "Inspirationals" from Fort Worth, Texas. At the time, Roger McDuff and Big John Hall were singing with them. We were also invited to sing in Evangel Temple in Fort Smith, Arkansas, where B. Owen Oslin was pastor. It was a large church with a balcony. I had never been in a church that large before. My home church would seat maybe one hundred and twenty-five. The church was filled to capacity the morning we were there. We were singing a song where I had the lead in the chorus. When it came to my part, my mind suddenly went blank. I couldn't remember my words; so, I just closed my eyes and lifted my hands like I was praising the Lord. When I lifted my hands, the congregation thought I was getting blessed, and they lifted their hands and began praising the Lord. The Lord began blessing in a wonderful way. Scott Taylor, our emcee, said, "I think we should sing it again." We started the song again and when it came time for me to sing, my mind was just as blank the second time as it was the first time, so, I closed my eyes and raised my hands the second time, and it worked just as well as it had the first time. The people began praising the Lord again. The quartet never let me forget that experience.

On one occasion we were invited to sing at the Oklahoma City Twin Hills Golf and Country Club. They wanted us to walk around and sing during the evening's activities. Bill Hedrick played his accordion while we sang that evening. They told us we could eat as much as we wanted as we sang. We took advantage of that opportunity because they kept bringing out fresh, hot, fried shrimp as well as many other delicious things. We enjoyed the evening! Just as we were getting ready to leave, they brought out one more platter of fried shrimp. I took a couple of napkins and filled them with shrimp and put them in my coat pockets as we left. After all, they had said we could eat all we wanted, and I wanted more shrimp! The guys never let me forget that experience either.

We traveled to Texas, Arkansas, and all over Oklahoma, singing and holding services in many different churches. More and more, I was given the opportunity to preach after we finished our singing. The pastors started calling me back to preach revivals and, as a result, I made the difficult decision to quit the quartet so I could do full time evangelistic work. I will always be indebted to the Sentries, and to the opportunity they gave me to sing and preach. I know that it was because of that open door, that the Lord opened other doors for me in the ministry. Churches always wanted us to come because we were all raising our kids, and when we came, we boosted their attendance. There were friendships made during that time that are still strong today.

My faith was growing as I saw the Lord open doors. I had watched Him supply our needs. I was learning more and more that I could depend on Him. It was a step of faith to leave the quartet and to begin full-time evangelistic ministry, but the Lord had proven Himself to be more than enough to Gretnia and me.

It was not easy in the beginning of my ministry. I discovered quickly that you do not begin at the top. I am somewhat concerned about many of our Bible School graduates today. They want to know what the package for their ministry will be before they accept the position offered them. I have never asked what a church was going to pay. The most important thing to me was whether or not it was the Lord's will for me to be there. I have always felt if it were the Lord's will for me to be there, that He would supply all of my needs. In our first few revivals there were anywhere from eight to thirteen in attendance. The offerings were not very good, but the Lord was moving in our midst, and people were being healed, saved, and filled with the Holy Spirit. Those were the most important things!

My father-in-law would allow me to work as a carpenter when I was not preaching revivals. Many times I would work eight to nine hours a day, and then go preach revivals at night. I was willing to do anything to keep preaching. I came to a period of time in the spring of 1961 that tested the very core of my faith. I went for three months without seeing anyone saved or filled or healed. I tried to pray and my prayers seemed to go unanswered. I tried to preach and it felt as though I was spitting cotton. I was not seeing any fruit to my ministry. I even began questioning my call into the ministry. It was during that period of time that I received a call from Rev. R.S. Stewart, pastor of Davenport Assembly of God Church. He wanted Gretnia and me for a revival. I was thrilled for the opportunity to preach.

Davenport was close enough to drive back and forth from Oklahoma City, so I decided to keep working for my father-in-law while I was in revival. I worked from 7:30 A.M. until 5:00 P.M. each day as a frame-in carpenter, then Gretnia would have a sandwich ready, and as soon as I got my shower and cleaned up, we would drive to church so I could preach. The services were scheduled for one week. I started on Sunday morning and preached until Friday. In that Friday evening service, a lady came forward and gave her heart to the Lord. I was thrilled. That was the first person in over three months who had responded to the invitation. The pastor told me that she had been the first person in over a year to be saved in the church.

Brother Stewart asked me after the service if we could continue with the revival the next week. Even though I did not have anything scheduled the following week, I told him I would pray about it and let him know Sunday morning when we arrived for the service. I prayed and prayed about going on with the revival, but I just didn't feel that it was what the Lord wanted me to do. When I shared those feelings with Brother Stewart, he couldn't understand why I wouldn't go on, but did agree to close the revival that Sunday night.

I had learned earlier in the year that I had better be sensitive to the Holy Spirit and what He wanted. I had been in revival in Gainesville, Texas in January. We had been having a wonderful meeting and the pastor wanted me to go on with the revival. I felt a check in my spirit about going on with the meeting, but the pastor really wanted it to continue, so I told him I would. It did not take long for me to know I had made a mistake. I found that I didn't have the liberty to preach as I had had earlier in the meeting. I could hardly wait for the revival to close. That experience was still fresh in my memory at the time of the Davenport revival and so I felt compelled to follow the Lord's leading.

I drove home from Davenport that Sunday night wondering why I hadn't felt impressed to continue the revival, especially since I didn't have anything else scheduled that following week. After all, it seemed that there had been a breakthrough in the moving of the Holy Spirit in my ministry. I was getting ready to go to work the next morning when the phone rang. I answered the phone and it was Brother R. L. Steger, pastor of Glad Tidings Assembly of God, in Oklahoma City. He told me that he had been praying and had felt impressed to call and see if I could come and preach for them on Wednesday night. I told him that I could. Brother Steger turned the service over to me that Wednesday evening, and, I hadn't even gotten out of the introduction of my message when the Holy Spirit fell. People started coming to the altar. Several were saved and filled with the Holy Spirit. I had a liberty to preach like I had never had before.

Brother Steger asked if I could come back Friday night for their mid-week service. I went back Friday night and the same thing happened again. I never finished my introduction, and, the Holy Spirit fell again. People were saved and filled with the Holy Spirit. Brother Steger asked me to come back Sunday morning. He said, "I think the Lord might be trying to tell us something and I don't want to miss His will." I went back Sunday morning and the same thing happened again. We wound up staying for the next four weeks. There were more than thirty saved and thirty filled with the Holy Spirit in those next four weeks. There were miracles of healing. The altar services were simply outstanding as the Holy Spirit moved in our midst. People were slain in the Spirit all across the front of the church. In those days we had no catchers and people were not pushed down. It was simply a sovereign move of the Holy Spirit.

One night while I was singing, I began singing in tongues. Sister Steger was part Cherokee Indian and when I finished the song, she asked me if I knew the Cherokee language. I told her that I did not know Cherokee. She told me that I had been singing in Cherokee and that she had understood everything I had sung.

That revival became the springboard for me in the ministry. Pastors heard about the revival and began calling to schedule me for revival in their churches. I never had to want for revivals again after that glorious experience.

I received my exhorter's papers from the Assemblies of God in 1959. Shortly after I received my papers, Rev. S. N. Greene, who had been my pastor in Healdton, called me. He told me that he felt I should have my papers with the Pentecostal Holiness Church since that is where I began my ministry. He informed me that he could help me get my minister's license with the PHC (which was a step higher than the exhorter's papers I had with the Assemblies of God) but that doing so would require me to drop my papers with the A/G. I decided to meet with the PHC conference board that summer and received my license to preach in the Pentecostal Holiness Church.

During the next several months, I was able to preach in Pentecostal Holiness churches as well as in Assemblies of God churches despite the fact I had dropped my exhorter's papers. The Lord had opened many doors for me. I was truly blessed to be able to preach in both denominations. Before long, however, I began feeling as though I had made a mistake in changing my papers from the Assemblies of God to the Pentecostal Holiness church. The more I prayed about it, the more I was sure I had made a mistake. I went to talk with Brother S. J. Scott, my pastor at Faith Tabernacle, and told him how I was feeling. He told me not to be afraid to do what the Holy Spirit was leading me to do. He told me he would sign my papers, recommending that I be reinstated by the Oklahoma District Council of the Assemblies of God, if that was what I wanted to do. I told him that that was what I felt the Lord wanted for my life.

I met with the District Board in the Sectional Council meeting for section nine. The meeting was held in February 1960, at the First Assembly of God, on South Pennsylvania in Oklahoma City. I will never forget climbing the stairs to the meeting room. When I walked in, there sat Rev. Robert E. Goggin, our District Superintendent, along with several other men from the District Board. Brother Goggin looked at me, and asked if I had made up my mind about where I wanted to preach. Did I want to be Pentecostal Holiness or did I want to be Assemblies of God? Then he informed me that they would not be doing this again and that I had better have made up my mind. I told them that I was sure about what the Lord wanted for my life, and that the Lord wanted me in the Assemblies of God. I have never been sorry about my decision and I have never looked back.

After the wonderful revival at Glad Tidings in Oklahoma City, I continued my studies for ordination. District Council was in October and I wanted to be finished with my studies so I could be ordained. The Lord helped me to accomplish my goal. I was ordained in the Assemblies of God on October 2, 1961. I will never forget that memorable night. Rev. James VanMeter preached my ordination. Rev. Carl McCoy was the district official who laid his hands on me and prayed for me. I can hardly comprehend the Lord calling me into the ministry. I look back where I came from and it blows my mind that He could use someone like me to preach His Word. I can never praise Him enough for all He has done for me!

Tammy, our daughter, was born on October 12, 1961. I had taken Gretnia to Baptist Memorial hospital when she began her labor. That proved to be a lengthy situation because she was in labor for twenty-one hours. But, it was worth it all, because the Lord gave us a beautiful baby girl, Tammy Lynn McGee. Tammy brought us great joy then and is still bringing us great joy today. We are extremely proud of both our children!

Gretnia and I had a 1959 Chevrolet that we drove to all of our revival meetings. It did not have air conditioning nor did it have an automatic transmission. We bought it strictly so we could get good gas mileage. A short time before Tammy was born, Gretnia was driving the car in Oklahoma City, when a soldier, who was home on leave, ran into her at an intersection. He hit her on the passenger's side, near the back door, causing considerable damage. Praise the Lord; it did not hurt Gretnia or the baby.

A few days later, Gretnia and I were driving on the south side of Oklahoma City, when all the traffic had to stop because of an approaching fire truck. We were the last car in the line of cars that had stopped. As the fire truck attempted to pass us they hit the left rear panel of our car, again causing considerable damage to our car. Our car looked terrible. There was damage on the right side of the car as well as the left side. We began praying about a new car, but as we looked around to see if we could trade our car in for a new one with air conditioning and automatic drive, we discovered they were all too expensive, especially with all the damage that had been done to our car.

We had discovered that the soldier who hit Gretnia did not have insurance, and then the Oklahoma City council members ruled that since the fire truck that hit us was going to a fire, they were not liable for the damage to our car. The Lord knows how to solve problems for us when we don't have the solutions though. That fact was soon proven in the most unusual way.

Gretnia and I had a revival meeting scheduled in Tulsa just after Tammy had been born. On our way to Tulsa and Lewis

Avenue Assembly of God church, we were driving across the Will Rogers turnpike when all of a sudden the fan belt on the car broke, and before I could stop, smoke began pouring out from under the hood of the car. The Lord was with us, however, because this happened right across the highway from the last stop on the turnpike and this particular place just happened to have a fan belt that fit our car. When we drove up in front of pastor John L. Human's home, he came out of his house, took one look at our car, and asked "How in the world did you get here with a mess like that?" The car smelled like it had been in a fire, and looked like it had been in a wreck. He immediately asked us if we would like to get another car. Then he proceeded to call a member of his church, Lee Eller, who had a car dealership, and told him he was bringing us to see him about a new car.

Gretnia and I had been looking at Chevrolets when we were trying to trade cars, but they had all been too expensive considering the damage done to our car. Lee Eller owned an Oldsmobile dealership. Oldsmobiles cost a lot more than Chevrolets. We had never dreamed of owning an Oldsmobile, but Lee Eller drove our car, then came back to us and told us what it would cost to trade for a 1961, four-door Dynamic 88 Oldsmobile with power seats, power steering, air conditioning, fully automatic, loaded with everything! The cost to trade was more than $2500 less than the Chevrolets we had been looking at.

The Lord had answered our prayers in a tremendous way. Brother Human told us later that Brother Eller had given us a big offering in letting us have the car for the price he gave us. We could never praise the Lord enough for all of His goodness to us. Our faith had been tested. The Lord was proving Himself to us in special ways. Our faith was growing!

There was a marvelous move of God in that two-week revival. Fifteen were saved and fifty-two received the baptism of the Holy Spirit. We had been having such a move of the Holy Spirit that there were a number of visitors attending. I remember one night in particular. The pastor of a large denominational church, which did not believe in speaking in tongues, came with several of his elders. One of the elders brought his sister with him to the meeting. The pastor had recognized the minister and his elders in the beginning of the service. As a result, the congregation had not entered into worship the way they had been doing. Evidently the visiting minister intimidated them.

When the pastor turned the service to me, I told the congregation I felt the Lord was trying to move in the service, but that they were not entering into worship. I asked if anyone was ashamed of the Lord. Then I said, "If you are not ashamed of the Lord, I want you to step out into the aisle when we begin singing, "When the Saints Go Marching In," and begin marching around the church." I asked the piano player to give me an E-flat chord and we began singing. It was not but just a few moments and all heaven broke loose. People began shouting and praising the Lord as a number of them received the baptism of the Holy Spirit. The piano player, who had never received the baptism of the Holy Spirit, fell off the piano bench, under the power of the Lord, speaking in tongues.

The delegation from the visiting church had joined in the march because they were not ashamed of the Lord. As they approached the front of the church, the sister of one of the elders, stopped in front of me and asked if the Lord would give her what the other people were receiving. I assured her that He would if she would raise her hands and begin to praise Him. She raised her hands and asked the Lord to fill her with the Holy Spirit. In just a few minutes, she began speaking in tongues. As she spoke in tongues, she went from one language to another. It was noticeable to everyone around her. It was a definite sign to her brother and the visiting minister that something supernatural had happened to her. The Lord had given her " **. . . divers kind of tongues . . .**" as stated in **1 Corinthians 12:10.**

I wish I could tell you that the visiting minister received the Holy Spirit that night, but he did not. However, two weeks later, he did receive the Holy Spirit, with the evidence of speaking in tongues. Our next revival was in Rockford, Illinois, at the First Assembly of God. Brother Scott told me before we left to be sure and say "Illinois," and not "Illinoise." He told me that if I said the latter that the folks there would tell me that there hadn't been any "noise" until I got there. We again had a mighty outpouring of the Holy Spirit. So many people were receiving the baptism of the Holy Spirit, that other churches in the area began sending people to First Assembly so their people could receive the Holy Spirit.

It was in that revival that Gretnia and I experienced the first outstanding miracle of healing in our ministry. The deaf were seated on the first row of the church so that they could receive sign language from the interpreter. I began praying for those who needed healing and a man came forward for prayer. When I prayed for him, he suddenly cried, "I can hear, I can hear!" I took my watch and put it next to his ears and he could hear the watch ticking. I had him turn and walk away from me as I was speaking and he could hear every word clearly. He sat at the back of the church the rest of the revival because he could hear everything clearly. Praise the Lord!

Many wonderful things occurred during that revival meeting. More than sixty people received the baptism of the Holy Spirit, several other people were healed along with the deaf man, and more than fifteen were saved. The Lord was moving in a mighty way, but we had to close the meeting and drive back home to Oklahoma City because Tammy, our daughter, had sensitive intestines and could not get any relief, even though we prayed nightly for her healing. It was strange because we prayed for others to be healed and they were healed, but we couldn't believe for Tammy's healing. It has always been easier for me to pray for others to be healed, because I always wanted the Lord to heal my family yesterday. It is hard to believe for your own family's healing. That's the reason we are to pray for one another.

We closed the revival on Sunday night and got up early

Monday morning and drove straight through to Oklahoma City. We felt we had to get Tammy home as quickly as possible. We took her to Faith Tabernacle on Wednesday night and asked Brother S. J. Scott, our pastor, to pray for her. The Lord instantly healed Tammy that night! She never had trouble with sensitive intestines after that.

I ended 1961 by beginning a revival on December 31st, at First Assembly of God in Enid, Oklahoma where Rev. Earl Kelly was pastor. I preached at the church that morning and then Sunday afternoon I preached a community-wide service at First Pentecostal Holiness church. That evening I preached the service back at First Assembly and then I preached the watch-night service at First Assembly. I preached four times that day and at midnight we had a Jericho march. It was a glorious way to end one year and to start a New Year!

That revival at Enid First Assembly of God lasted the entire month of January 1962. The temperature never got above zero degrees that entire month, but we had great crowds every night. In fact, we started having services at 10:00 A.M. each morning as well. People were filled with the Holy Spirit in those morning services as we gathered to worship the Lord. Two of Rev. Earl Kelly's sons were called into the ministry during that revival meeting.

I was preaching one Sunday morning during that revival meeting when suddenly an older gentleman suffered a massive heart attack. An ambulance was called and they took him to the hospital. The church prayed for him as he was being taken to the hospital. I finished my message, gave the invitation, and prayed for those who came forward. After I had finished the altar service some people from the church took me to the hospital. When we arrived at the hospital we were told that the man had passed away and had been dead about ten minutes. I asked if we could pray. I began praying for his wife, and then I asked the Lord to heal her husband. I'll never forget it as long as I live, because the nurse who had covered the man with a sheet, suddenly shouted,

"He's alive! He's alive!" The man had been healed! He had thrown the sheet away from his face, and had sat up in bed.

He shared how the Lord had come to take him as the doctors were working on him. He said he saw the doctors tell his wife that he had died and that there was nothing more that could be done. He said he saw his wife as she began crying. He told us the Lord began taking him up and soon he was soaring through the sky. He said he began hearing beautiful singing and could see the brightness of that glorious city as they began drawing close to heaven. Then suddenly, the Lord asked him if he had any sheaves to lie at His feet. He told the Lord that he didn't think that he had any sheaves as he looked at his empty hands. The Lord told him He would give him a chance to win souls because He was being asked to heal him. He told us the Lord brought him back to the hospital and he could see all of us praying for him. That is when he threw the sheet off his face and sat up in the bed.

The hospital kept him for three more days, running all kinds of tests on him, but could find nothing wrong with him. He then came back to the revival meeting and shared the story I have just shared with you. People came from everywhere to the revival after he shared his testimony. He was a car dealer in Enid. He began calling people with whom he had done business and began sharing what the Lord had done for him. He led a number of people to the Lord. He lived a number of years after that experience.

I will never forget that revival meeting! The Lord had proven Himself over and over again. He had taught us in **Matthew 17:20, " . . . If ye have faith as a grain of mustard seed, ye shall say unto this mountain, Remove hence to yonder place; and it shall remove; and nothing shall be impossible unto you."** Impossible things had become possible! He was the Lord of the miraculous!

The beginning of 1963 proved to be another exciting adventure for Gretnia and me and our two children, Kenny and

Tammy. Dan and Bonnie Sheaffer invited us to come to Miami, Oklahoma, to be their associate pastors. That proved to be a wonderful experience for us. I feel I learned a lot under the leadership of Dan Sheaffer. He was and is one of the greatest preachers I have ever heard. He is currently the pastor of Crossroads Cathedral in Oklahoma City. He helped me expand my ministry. He gave me the chance to direct his choir and to learn how to operate the office machines. He also taught me the art of preparing sermons. In addition, I had the privilege of helping him with his radio broadcast. He helped me in spreading my wings even more. I could see how my faith was being increased in accepting new and greater responsibilities.

Bonnie Sheaffer is an excellent cook. She taught Gretnia how to make delicious lasagna. Tammy, our daughter, was only about fifteen months old at the time, but she fell in love with Bonnie's lasagna. She still loves it to this day.

Gretnia and I had gone to Miami with the understanding with Dan and Bonnie that if we missed the evangelistic field too much we would resign and go back in the field. After three months we resigned and moved back to Oklahoma City and started preaching revivals again. We will never forget the many wonderful experiences with the Sheaffers and the great church in Miami.

1964 began with us in revival at Grace Assembly of God in Oklahoma City where J. D. Keen was pastor. We had been in revival with him in 1961 when Tammy was born. In fact, Brother Keen nicknamed Tammy, "Gracie," because she was born during that revival. Brother Keen talked to me one night and told me that First Assembly of God church in El Reno was open. He told me that he had been pastor there and that he knew the secretary and treasurer and would be glad to talk to him if I would be interested in the church. I told him I didn't think I would be interested because I was perfectly happy doing evangelistic work. Little did I know what the Lord had in store for Gretnia and me. He was getting ready to expand our ministry and increase our faith even more.

Chapter Six
OUR FIRST CHURCH

I could not get away from what Brother Keen had told me about the church in El Reno. Every time I got down to pray for the next several days I kept thinking about El Reno, El Reno, El Reno. Finally, I told Brother Keen how I had been feeling. I told him I would like to check into the church. He told me the name of the secretary and treasurer, Art Mitchell, and told me he would call him for me. We made an appointment to meet Brother Mitchell at his home.

The night before we were to meet I had a dream. In my dream Gretnia and I went into a home and met the people and talked to them about becoming pastors at their church. The next day Gretnia and I drove to El Reno to meet the Mitchells. When I knocked on the door, Art and Cleta Mitchell answered the door and invited us into their home. I will never forget the feeling I had when I saw them and the inside of their home. **They were the very people I had seen in my dream and their house was the home I had seen in my dream!** I knew then that the Lord had His hand in our being there.

We talked about the church and then talked about what we had been doing in our ministry. I told him we had been doing evangelistic work our entire ministry. I told him about Brother Keen telling me about the church and, how the Lord had dealt with me over the next several days about inquiring about the church. He told me they had an older minister scheduled to come to the church Sunday morning to preach, but that I could come

Sunday night. The church would then vote on the two of us to see who would become pastor.

Brother Mitchell told me about the financial arrangements for the pastor. The previous pastor had been receiving 100% of the tithes. The church would then receive a Sunday evening offering to pay the bills of the church. The church was more than three months behind in their bills at that time. I told Brother Mitchell that I would not be interested in that arrangement, but that I would propose the pastor receive 75% of the tithes and the church receive 25%. He asked if I thought that Gretnia and I could make it financially with that arrangement. I assured him that we could. I was taking a step of faith because that is what I felt the Lord wanted me to do. It is interesting where the walk of faith will lead you. The Lord wanted me to trust Him that the 75% would eventually be more than the 100%.

Gretnia and I agreed to come back to El Reno Sunday night and see what the Lord had in store for us. The next day Brother Mitchell called and told us that the older minister had called and told him that he would not be coming to preach Sunday morning. He wanted to know if we could come and preach both services, and then told us that they would vote on us after the evening service.

Gretnia, Kenny, Tammy, and I drove to El Reno that Sunday morning wondering what the Lord's plan was for our lives. It was almost time for Kenny to start to school yet we had not really thought that much about how that was going to work out with us traveling the way we were. The Lord always works out His will in our lives if we will just let Him.

I preached on the subject, "Behold, A Greater Than Solomon," from **Matthew 12:42**, in the Sunday morning service. I had a lot of liberty in preaching both services that day. The Holy Spirit moved in a special way. The attendance that morning was 63. After the evening service the church was called to order for the business meeting.

I only had one question asked that evening. I was not

asked if I were licensed or ordained in the Assemblies of God, or how long I had been in the ministry. I wasn't even asked if I were saved or filled with the Holy Spirit. The only question I was asked was, "How old are you?" I told the person who asked the question that that was not the important thing. The important thing was, "Is this the perfect will of God?" That is always the most important thing for the church as well as for the minister. The most important thing is not "How much will the church pay?" or "What is the package I will receive?"

The vote was cast and we received all the votes but two. The people who did not vote for us thought we were too young to be their pastors. I was the ripe old age of 27!

The church had a parsonage, which was next door to the church. When we were taken over to see the parsonage it was evident that it needed a lot of cleaning and repair. The carpet was old and dirty and the inside of the house needed painting. Gretnia's dad was a builder and knew a man who would sell us carpet for builder's cost. He called Doyle Brimberry and he came over and measured the house for new carpet. We were excited about our new home with new carpet. Gretnia and I were paying for the carpet because the church did not have the money at the time.

I received a call from one of the board members a few nights later around 2:30 A.M. He told me that the parsonage was on fire. We drove as quickly as we could to El Reno because we were still living in Oklahoma City at the time. When we arrived at the parsonage we were told the carpet layers had left the carpet lying over the floor furnace, and that the carpet had caught on fire. The fire had not spread quickly, but had caused a lot of smoke damage to the house.

That all proved to be a blessing of the Lord because the church had insurance on the parsonage and the carpet company also had insurance. Since the burning carpet had caused all the smoke damage, the insurance paid to have the carpet replaced, and to have the entire house repainted. We were able to select our own colors. When it was all over, we had a new paint job and new carpet, and it didn't cost us a thing. The Lord gave us a tremendous blessing! He was working in our behalf. He was showing us that if we would move in His will, He would open the windows of heaven and give us the desires of our hearts. Our faith was growing!

It was a special time when we moved into the parsonage after the fire. Everything looked new and smelled new. When we would go to bed at night, we put gospel records on to play. That's the way we went to sleep, night after night.

The church was in need of a lot of repair as well. The bathrooms were dirty and the sanctuary needed a lot of TLC. The basement needed a lot of cleaning as well. It is amazing what a lot of elbow grease and a number of willing hands can accomplish. It wasn't long until the bathrooms were usable again, the nursery was in great shape, the basement was clean, and the sanctuary was ready for worship.

Within the first two months of our pastorate, all of the church's bills were paid and our income of 75% of the tithes turned out to be more than the previous pastor's income of 100% of the tithes. We were having a wonderful move of the Holy Spirit and the church was growing. During our time at the church we cut the percentage of our income two times. When we resigned and left the church we were receiving 65% of the tithes and the church was receiving 35%.

Sister Ruth Wilson began attending our church not too long after we became pastors. Her son, J. P., and his wife, JoElla, owned the Cherokee Trading Post just west of town. Sister Wilson had come to stay with them and help in the trading post. J. P. and JoElla had not been in church for a while so I began visiting them, encouraging them to come regularly. JoElla began coming, bringing Sherry, their daughter, and Randy, their son. When JoElla first began coming, she had to get up a number of times and take Sherry out to the nursery, because church was new to her little girl. JoElla's persistence paid off quickly though.

Before long Sherry became accustomed to the church and did not have to be taken out anymore. I wish that there were more mothers like JoElla Wilson. All it takes is a little patience and training with children and they will settle down in church.

I had quite a time trying to visit J. P. He would see me driving out I-40 on my way to visit him, and would disappear from the trading post. It was evident he didn't want to talk to me, but I knew he was running from the Lord and I was not going to be discouraged. I decided one day to go out the old Highway 66 that came in on the backside of the trading post. When I drove up to the trading post he was still there. He had not seen me coming. My plan had worked. I began talking to him and invited him to church. J. P. began coming with JoElla and the kids and it was not long before he gave his heart to the Lord.

Ruth Wilson was a godly woman with a lot of wisdom. Gretnia and I would go to the trading post to visit her and would ask her to share her godly wisdom with us. El Reno was our first church as I have stated before, and Sister Wilson's talks were invaluable to us. She had great spiritual insight in the things of the Lord and gave us a lot of wisdom in dealing with people. Gretnia and I will forever be indebted to Sister Wilson. I had the privilege several years later of preaching her funeral.

Our faith was growing through listening to the wise counsel of godly people: people who walked the walk, lived the life, and shared their life experiences. It was needful in our maturing process in the Lord. There are too many today who think they know it all. They don't feel they need help or counsel from anyone.

By the end of our first year at El Reno it was evident that we needed a new church building. Gretnia and I had been voted in for a one-year term, so the first item of business in our annual business meeting in 1965 was a vote on whether or not we would be retained as pastors. We received a new three-year term on a unanimous vote. I then presented the plans for a new church building. The plans required that we sell the old church and purchase new property. I wasn't quite ready for what happened next. The church body voted unanimously, not only to relocate and build the new church, but to also build a new parsonage. A new parsonage was an added blessing that day.

In February 1965 the final transactions were completed for the new location of the church which was to be built in a new residential section of town. The new address would be 1701 - 1731 South Jensen. We were able to secure an entire city block for the new church. The plans for the new church were similar to Bethel Temple Assembly of God in Midwest City, Oklahoma. The church would seat about 250, which was about twice the seating capacity of the old church. The plans called for a new kitchen, evangelist's quarters, and ample classrooms for the size of the sanctuary.

I had to secure the loan to build the buildings and get the zoning changed for the property. (In order for us to build on the city block we had to have the city close the alley which ran through the middle of the property.) I began trying to secure the loan to build the church through banks and savings and loan facilities in El Reno. However, no one in El Reno would loan us the money to build our new church. The payment on the old church had only been $72 a month and evidently the church had not had a good reputation in paying their bills. Whatever the reason, I could not find a loan in El Reno.

I drove over to Weatherford, Oklahoma and met with Custer County Federal Savings and Loan. I was able to secure the loan to build our new church and pay off the old church loan. The new payment was going to be $800 a month. I had the money to build; now I needed the zoning changed so we could start building. The zoning proved to be quite a challenge! The city had decided not to close the alley and not to give us the zoning change. It turned out that while I was having the abstract being brought up to date, we discovered the city had put the main sewer line across the property we were buying, and had not had the permission of the owner to do so. The city had never obtained an easement for the sewer line! When I discovered what they had done, I went before the city council and told them I would allow them to keep the sewer line where it was if they would close the alley for us. They agreed to do so and, also gave us the zoning change we had requested.

There was a family living down the street from where the church was going to be built that was fighting us every inch of the way. I found out that they were backslidden Assembly of God people. They claimed that there would be too much traffic coming onto Jensen Street if the city allowed us to have a driveway coming out of our property. They just simply did not want the church to be built there.

I had met with the County Commissioner and he had told me he would bring equipment and cut the driveway for us and level the property off so we could put the paving down and it would not cost us anything. We were blessed then because those things are not permitted today. I met the last time before the city council and they informed us that we could not cut the driveway and come onto Jensen Street with the traffic. The council chamber was packed with our people as well as many others from the city that night. I then told the city council that they would have to sue the church and take us to court, because we were going to do it anyway. I told them what the County Commissioner had told me and that he was willing to start immediately. I told them we had the money and the plans were ready and we were going to get started building. The whole chamber erupted in applause!

I knew that I had prayed and prayed about what the Lord wanted us to do, and I felt that He was leading me in my decisions, so I had a peace in my heart. I know that my faith was growing through the whole process. He had led me to the right place to secure the loan, and He had led me in dealing with the city council. Faith can move mountains! There had been mountains of obstacles, and yet the Lord had helped us through every one of them.

At long last it was time to start building. I had told the

church that I would help them in the building of the church. I would supervise everything if they would help me do the work. I had learned how to build by doing that kind of work with my father-in-law all the years that I had been in the evangelistic field. I secured the use of a ditch-digging machine from the manager of a lumber company and set the day to dig the footings of the church and the parsonage. We planned on staking it out, digging, setting the steel, and pouring the footings all in one day. My brother-in-law, Mickey Caldwell, had agreed to come over from Oklahoma City and help me do the work.

Mickey and I got to the location early that morning. We worked all day, just the two of us, and as we were pouring the last of the footings, a couple of the men from the church came by to see how we were doing. It was almost 8:30 P.M. Later, I called all the men together and told them that I was willing to help them, but that they would have to help, because this was their church as well. I told them that if they could not help me, then we would pay someone to do the work. My father-in-law, Tommy Grant, offered to do all the work for cost—plus 10%. The church voted to have Tommy build the church. He brought his men and sub-contractors and the work continued immediately.

It was so exciting seeing the church being built. The people were excited. Excitement breeds excitement. The church was growing. People were being saved and filled with the Holy Spirit. We were having wonderful services in the old church, but we were anxious to get into our new church. Finally, everything was finished, and we had our dedication in January 1966. It was an exciting day!

The church had been organized on October 1, 1932 at the home of Claude Siler, under the direction of Pastor D. B. Jaggers. The first meeting place had been at the Wallace garage, then at various other buildings and sites, including the Canadian County Courthouse, before church leaders were finally being able to secure property and a building on West Wade Street in El Reno. The church had remained at this location until January

1949, at which time it purchased the Nazarene Church building and parsonage at 702 S. Bickford Street. The church had then occupied the old Nazarene Church building for seventeen years prior to our moving into the new church building and parsonage on South Jensen in January 1966. It was truly an exciting day!

1966 proved to be both an exciting and challenging year. We broke the all-time attendance record with 169 people present. The Lord had given us wonderful growth from the initial 63 on our first Sunday. We had a wonderful revival with brothers, John and Robert Stevens. They were the first ones to stay in our new evangelist's quarters.

The payment for our new church was $800 a month. That may not seem like very much today, but then, it represented a large jump from our $72 a month payment on the old church. We decided to start making and selling peanut brittle in order to help make the payments. I had a wonderful recipe which I had received from one of our missionaries. We would meet in the new church once a week to make the peanut brittle. That proved to be a great time of fellowship for the entire church. Each batch would produce three packages of peanut brittle. Each package sold for 75 cents. We would make enough peanut brittle to clear more than $800 a month. In fact, we could not make enough to fill all the orders. I didn't want us to work more than one night a week. We made the peanut brittle from October through March, making enough money during that period of time to make all our church payments.

One of our families came to me one week and asked if we could make "prune brittle" for them. I had never heard of "prune brittle." I told them that we could. The next week when we began making our brittle, instead of putting peanuts in one of the batches, I put in prunes. We pulled it as it was cooling, just like we did when we put the peanuts in it. Amazingly, it turned out just fine. The family loved it. In fact, they gave us $5 for the batch, instead of $2.25.

It always seems that when the Lord has been blessing

and things are going smoothly that the devil begins working. That certainly appeared to be the case in the church. Art Slaton was our Sunday School Superintendent. He was also employed by the city of El Reno as the Superintendent of the Water Department. Brother Slaton and I would meet each Wednesday at 6:00 P.M. and go over the plans for the coming Sunday. On one particular Wednesday however, when 6:00 P.M. came, he was not there. That was not like Brother Slaton because he was always on time. I waited for fifteen minutes and called his home. Sister Slaton told me that he had not come in from work, but that she would call me as soon as he came in. Another fifteen minutes passed and she called and told me that he was still not in and that she was worried because it was not like him to be late and not call to let her know why he was late. I called her just before church and told her I would come out as soon as church was over and we would try to find him.

I called again after church and discovered that he still was not home. I called the sheriff and asked him to meet me at the Slaton's home. When we arrived Sister Slaton told us that Brother Slaton sometimes worked on their acreage with his tractor and that she thought that that is where he had gone that afternoon. We found out from the people at the water department that he had indeed left the water plant early and had gone somewhere else, but that they did not know where he had gone for sure.

The sheriff and I drove out to the Slaton's property and began driving across the land with the vehicle's lights on. We saw the tractor stopped in the middle of the field. When we approached the tractor we saw Brother Slaton under the wheel of the tractor. Evidently he had hit a large root in the ground and it had thrown him off the tractor and he landed under the wheel. He had been dead for quite some time. It was very difficult having to tell Sister Slaton and their daughter, Jacque, that Brother Slaton was dead.

The church was packed to capacity for his funeral. The mayor, the city manager, the council members, and many city employees were in attendance. The church seated 250 and every seat was filled. The people from the community were very complimentary about our new church. I had wanted them to come to the new church, but not under those circumstances.

Later that year Gretnia, Kenny, Tammy, and I were in Oklahoma City on a Friday night watching a wrestling match at Putman City's gym when I received an emergency call over the public address system. I was told that the Russell Wood family from our church in El Reno had been in a bad car wreck and that they were being taken to St. Anthony's hospital in Oklahoma City. I went immediately to St. Anthony's hospital and arrived just as the first ambulance was pulling up with Marjorie and Paula Wood in it. I found out that the family had been traveling on the Turner Turnpike on their way to Bartlesville when a truck passed them just as they were approaching a bridge. The force of wind generated by the truck had pushed their car sideways and had caused them to hit the bridge head-on.

Marjorie had been driving the car and Paula and Mary, two of her daughters, had been in the front seat with her, along with her husband, Russell. Johnny, Delaine, and Jimmy, the other children, had been in the back seat. Marjorie and Paula had been the most seriously injured. That is why they had been in the first ambulance. One half of Marjorie's face was gone, and Paula had been crushed, sustaining multiple internal injuries. Mary had been thrown into the rear view mirror. The rear view mirror had caught her right under her nose and had literally cupped her mouth out of her face. Russell had sustained two broken legs. Delaine had been thrown from the back seat, through the front windshield, and had literally been scalped. Johnny and Jimmy had received broken arms and multiple wounds. They all had many wounds.

The hospital staff started working diligently tending to their wounds and injuries. I was asked to stay with the family while they were being treated. The kids were taken into X-ray and were calm as long as I was praying with them. They all responded as long as I was there. I was in the emergency room while they were receiving their stitches for their wounds. I never left the hospital for 25 hours. I left only after Marjorie and Paula had passed away. It was about 1:00 A.M. Sunday morning when I finally got home. It was not easy to preach that Sunday morning. I am glad to report that all the rest of the family eventually recovered from their injuries.

You learn through experiences like that just how much you need and depend on the Lord. It is during times like that that your faith grows. I was learning that you don't just awaken one morning and find that you have all the faith you need. Instead, you receive more and more faith as you learn through experiences. You learn that you need the Lord and that He is always there as **Psalms 46:1** states, **"God is our refuge and strength, a very present help in trouble."**

That fall, Marcus Alexander, a good friend of mine who was pastor of Bethel Assembly of God in Duncan, Oklahoma at that time, called and asked if I could come and preach a revival for him. I told him that I would be glad to come but that I would have to be home to preach on Sunday mornings. Real revival broke out and we went on in the revival for three weeks. That proved to be a time of refreshing for me after all the tragedies we had had in the church.

As we were approaching Christmas, a lady from the church stopped by to see Gretnia and me, and asked if we could give an offering to help one of our church families who had not received their Social Security check. I told her we would be glad to help but that we had just paid our car payment and did not have any money until we received our check from the church. We were flat broke! She told us not to worry about it because she would put some money in for us and we could give it back to her after we received our check. We told her we appreciated her doing that because we knew the other family needed the money. When we received our check from the church we gave her the money she had given for us. What I did not know at that time was that when she left our house and went to others in the church, she told them that we had not given in the offering. Shortly thereafter I began to notice that the tithes were dropping and the building fund offering was increasing. I could not understand why. I did not find out until later.

In 1967, Marcus Alexander, whom I have mentioned earlier, called me one Sunday after our morning service and told me that he had resigned, and that the church had voted unanimously for me to be their pastor. That was not the first time that that had happened. Rev. Willie Lowder, who had been pastor of Bethel Assembly of God before Brother Alexander, had resigned several years before, and had called and told me that the church had voted us in unanimously as their pastor. I had been to the church back then singing with the Sentries quartet, and had preached several times for Brother Lowder. I had felt honored that I would be asked to be their pastor, but I had not felt that it was the Lord's will for my life at that time.

So, when Brother Alexander called, I told him that I would come and meet with the board members and give them a decision. As I prayed, I wondered if the Lord was speaking to me, since this was the second time that I had been voted in unanimously at that church. I met with the board and we discussed the church and their feelings about Gretnia and me becoming their pastors. Bethel was about twice the size of the congregation in El Reno and the pay they offered was considerably more than what my percentage was in El Reno. It all seemed to be the right thing to do, so I told them I would take the church. However, I told them we could not come until the General Council of the Assemblies of God in Long Beach, California was over, which would be in August. I went back to El Reno and resigned. I told them that we would not be leaving until after the General Council in August.

I had scheduled a revival in Holtville, California before the General Council. Every time I would get down to pray, I had an uneasy feeling about going to Duncan. That feeling persisted throughout the entire revival. That feeling persisted all during the General Council. As we were driving back from General Council, I knew that I had made a mistake. The Lord wanted me to stay in El Reno.

When we got back home I called the board at Bethel and told them what I had been experiencing and that I would not be coming to their church. When some members of our family found out that we were not going to Duncan, they thought that I was making a big mistake. In fact, there were quite a few people who felt that way. I told them that I had to do what I felt the Lord wanted me to do. That is where your faith plays an important role. I then met with the board at El Reno and reapplied for the church. Since I had resigned, to be voted back in, would require a two-thirds vote.

It was during this time that I found out why the tithes had dropped and the building fund had increased. When the lady who had come to receive the offering for the needy family, had left our house, she had told people that we had not given in the offering, and that had offended many of the people. That is when they began holding their tithes and giving in the building fund. Thankfully I was able to tell the people what had happened and we were voted back in as pastors. The Lord continued to bless our ministry in El Reno after we were voted back in. The tithes increased and things got back to normal. The devil will always try to upset the apple cart if he can. He had tried to bring dissension into the church and had succeeded for a time, but the Lord was able to get it all worked out.

This proved to be yet another time for our faith to be tested. We were continuing to grow in our faith. Sometimes you have to be tested, to learn that the Lord is allowing certain things to happen. In **Job 13:15,** Job cried out when he was being tested, **"Though he slay me, yet will I trust in him . . ."** Our responsibility to the Lord was to trust Him. After all, **Psalms 37:23** states, **"The steps of a good man are ordered by the Lord: and he delighteth in his way."**

If Gretnia and I had taken the church in Duncan, we may never have known why the change had occurred in El Reno. The Lord allowed us to go through that test, and then brought us back to the church, so He could help us get the problem straightened out. As a result, the El Reno church was made stronger and we learned a valuable lesson.

El Reno was a special place for Gretnia and me and our two children. Kenny had started to school our first year there and was in the third grade by the time we were voted back in. Tammy was just starting in preschool at that time. Since our pastorate began we had relocated the church and had gone through a major building program. We had seen the church break the attendance record. We had experienced wonderful revivals and a number had been saved and filled with the Holy Spirit. We had had our share of tests and trials, as is the case in most ministries. But, I could see how the Lord had been with us and had brought us through them all. I knew that I had grown a great deal in my faith life. It was amazing the many things that the Lord had taught me.

One Saturday night in February 1968, I had gone to the church to pray and to prepare for the Sunday morning service. While I was praying, I began feeling the Lord was through with us at the church and that it was time to resign. I continued to pray, but I could not get away from that feeling. I went back to the parsonage and told Gretnia what I was feeling. She told me to do what I felt the Lord wanted me to do. So, I went back to the church and prayed and prayed, until I was sure that that is what the Lord wanted me to do. I wrote out my letter of resignation and read it to the church at the end of my message the next morning.

I did not have a church to go to, nor did I have any revivals scheduled at that time. I just knew that the Lord was through with me at El Reno. It was amazing what happened the following week. I booked enough revivals for the rest of the year within a week's time. The Lord truly had His hand on us.

We moved back to Oklahoma City and started our revivals. The Lord was opening doors for us. It was not long until the Lord opened doors for us in California. We had revivals scheduled in San Bernardino, where Louis Hoff was pastor; in Sacramento, where Clyde Henson was pastor; and in Bell Gardens, where Rev. S. E. Bowler was pastor. Those were the three largest churches in California at that time.

It was not long after that, that I was working on a church that Gretnia's dad was building. (He was good to let me work when I was in between revivals.) I was working on the roof of the church one day when Rev. S. J. Scott, pastor of Faith Tabernacle, drove up and wanted to talk to me. He told me that he had been praying and that he felt that he should ask me if I would be interested in coming on staff with him at Faith Tabernacle. I told him that I had just booked the three revivals I have just mentioned and that I would have to pray about it. I told him that I would let him know on the following Sunday.

I began to diligently seek the Lord. Going to Faith Tabernacle was perhaps the last thing I would have thought of doing at that time. However, over the next several days, every time I prayed, I felt that that is what the Lord wanted me to do. So I met with Brother Scott that following Sunday morning and told him that I felt it was the Lord's will for us to come to Faith Tabernacle. I never realized just what the Lord had in store for us!

Chapter Seven
YEARS AT FAITH TABERNACLE

Gretnia and I became the associate pastors at Faith Tabernacle in June of 1968. It seemed like a dream to us: to come back to the church where we were married and had begun our ministry almost twelve years before. It would indeed be a privilege to work with Brother and Sister Scott. After all, he was the one who had married us and had dedicated our two children. He was the one who had given me the opportunity to work with the youth. He was the one who had prayed for Tammy when she was healed of sensitive intestines. He had been invaluable to me in the ministry.

Brother Scott had often taken me to different minister's meetings to introduce me to other ministers, trying to help me get speaking engagements. As we drove to and from each place, he would ask me to quote Scriptures with him. He told me he would quote a Scripture and then I was to quote a Scripture. We would see who could quote the most Scriptures. I never did win in that little game!

Rev. Jerry B. Walker came for a revival shortly after we became associates at Faith Tabernacle. During the revival he received an offering for Gretnia and me to go to the Holy Land with Brother Scott in November of that same year, 1968. The trip to the Holy Land was a dream come true. I had always wanted to go, but had never had the money. Now, the Lord had made it possible. He was honoring our faith in Him and our obedience to His will. Faith can move mountains!

I prayed before Gretnia and I left on the trip for the Lord to help me remember what we would experience on the trip. To this day, I can still pull out the slides and tell you about every single one of them. The feelings I had then are still just as real today!

It was exciting as we boarded the plane in Oklahoma City. We flew from Oklahoma City to Dallas, from Dallas to New York City, and then from New York City on to Cairo, Egypt. Brother Scott had checked our luggage from Oklahoma City all the way to Cairo, which was our last stop, so we would not have to worry with it in New York City. When we arrived in Cairo, we all waited for our luggage to come off the plane so we could go through customs, but Gretnia's luggage evidently had not made the trip, because she never got her luggage. We reported that fact to the authorities in Cairo, and they assured us that it would be on the next flight. Her luggage was not on the next flight, however. In fact, her luggage never showed up the entire trip!

Gretnia had worn a beautiful all-wool suit and high heel shoes for our trip. We visited the pyramids, the Sphinx, rode camels, and did our sightseeing with her wearing the same clothes and shoes. Fortunately though there were several ladies on the trip with us who later let her wear some of their clothes. At least she didn't have to wear the same clothes all the time!

Egypt was truly a fascinating place. The Alabaster Mosque was interesting. You had to wash your hands, feet, and eyes, as well as take off your shoes before you could enter. Their belief was that before you worshipped, you must wash your hands, in case you had handled something you should not have handled. You must wash your feet, in case you had gone somewhere you should not have gone. You must wash your eyes, in case you had seen something you should not have seen. The inside was absolutely beautiful. Marble flooring, beautiful furnishings, and gold fixtures were everywhere.

It was absolutely awesome arriving in Israel. There I was a young man from Healdton, Oklahoma, in the very place where my wonderful Lord had lived. The Lord was leading me on a very exciting trip.

Every place we visited was special. We went to Bethlehem and saw the Church of the Nativity, built over the stable where Jesus was born. We visited the Mosque in Hebron where Sarah, Abraham, Isaac, Rebecca, Jacob, and Leah were buried.

And I will never forget when we visited the traditional locations of the tomb of David and the Upper Room. We had a diverse group; which included Methodists, Baptists, Catholics, Episcopalians and those of us who were Pentecostal. We also had a tour guide who was an atheist. He had informed us that he knew all the facts about the Holy Land, but that he just didn't believe in God or Jesus. He also informed us that we would not have time to tarry in the Upper Room because other groups were waiting to get into the room.

After he had given us the information about the Upper Room, Brother Scott asked if we could have a moment of silent prayer. He said, "Yes." That is all it took! In just a few moments, the Holy Spirit fell! The Pentecostals were praising the Lord, speaking in tongues, and all the others were weeping and praising the Lord. It literally felt like there was a wind blowing in that place. I still get cold chills just thinking about that wonderful experience. Heaven came down and everyone was getting blessed. The Holy Spirit is the common denominator of every believer. I could truly imagine how it must have felt on the Day of Pentecost! Since that time, Gretnia and I have had the privilege of going back to the Holy Land, eleven more times. We have had the same glorious experience each time we have gone back. Heaven comes down when we get into the Upper Room!

We then visited the old city of Jerusalem. Within the walls were the Pool of Bethesda and the Via Dolorosa (the 14 Stations of the Cross). Outside the Damascus gate, we then went to Mount Calvary, where our blessed Lord was crucified. Then we went to the Garden Tomb where Jesus was buried. Our group was given the privilege of entering the empty tomb. That is not permitted today, so we were especially blessed. A ray of sunlight was shining through a hole in the tomb. The light was falling at the place where the head of Jesus would have been laid. The presence of the Lord was so real that everyone began weeping and praising the Lord. We had witnessed, with our own eyes, the fact that Jesus was not there! He's alive! Again, the Holy Spirit moved on every denomination represented there in the tomb. We all had communion and worshipped the Lord.

We visited the Garden of Gethsemane, where horticulturists have verified that the olive trees in the garden date back to the time of Christ. I knelt by the side of an old olive tree and prayed for the Lord to lead me in the course of my life. I could see the Kidron Valley and the Eastern Gate from where I was kneeling and praying. I knew that the Eastern Gate was closed and will remain closed until the Lord returns to earth and walks through the gate. The Bible was alive with reality!

We then went to the area spoken of in **Matthew 26:39** which says, **"And he went a little farther, and fell on his face, and prayed, saying, O my Father, if it be possible, let this cup pass from me: nevertheless not as I will, but as thou wilt."** A little farther, where Jesus knelt and prayed, is where the victory of the Cross was won! Had Jesus not surrendered to the perfect will of God there, He would never have gone to the cross. But, Praise the Lord, He went a little farther and submitted to the perfect will of the Father!

A church had been built over the area, but we could go to the place where tradition says Jesus had knelt when He prayed that prayer. I remember praying "Lord, not my will in my life, but your will be done." That simple prayer, in that place, had special meaning to me. I can testify that the Lord has led me on an exciting journey.

We drove to the Mount of Olives and the place from which our Lord ascended back into Heaven. Before He ascended, He spoke these words found in **Acts 1:8 "But ye shall receive power, after that the Holy Ghost is come upon you: and ye** shall be witnesses unto me both in Jerusalem, and in all Judea, and in Samaria, and unto the uttermost part of the earth."

Can you imagine what the disciples must have been thinking as they experienced the events described in **Acts 1:10–11, "And while they looked stedfastly toward heaven as he went up, behold two men stood by them in white apparel; Which also said, Ye men of Galilee, why stand ye gazing up into heaven? This same Jesus, which is taken up from you into heaven shall so come in like manner as ye have seen him go into heaven."** Praise the Lord! The Lord is coming back again!

We proceeded to the Kidron Valley, passing the tombs of Absalom, St. James, and Zechariah. We saw the tunnel dug by Hezekiah and visited the Pool of Siloam, where the blind man in **John 9:1–11** was healed.

We then drove north, through the plains of Shechem, and visited Jacob's well, referred to in the fourth chapter of John. Next we proceeded to Sebastia, the ancient Samaria, founded by Omri, which was the first capital of the Northern Kingdom. Samaria is where the palaces of Jezebel were located and where Salome is said to have danced to have John the Baptist beheaded.

We stopped at the Jordan River where it empties out of the Sea of Galilee, and had a water baptismal service. I had asked Brother Scott to baptize Gretnia and me in the Jordan River. There were a number of us who were baptized that day. That was such a meaningful service to me. I had wanted to be baptized in the same Jordan River in which Jesus had been baptized. I will never forget the feeling of that great day!

We enjoyed a boat ride from Tiberias to Capernaum. I'll never forget the experience I had as we were going across the Sea of Galilee. I could envision the Lord as He came down from the mount where He had been praying, and, as He approached the water's edge, He never broke stride, but began walking on the water to the disciples. The Bible had literally come alive again, just as had been the case many times before on the trip.

We left Tiberias and went to Nazareth, the boyhood home of Jesus. Megiddo, the Chariot City of Solomon, was next on our trip. It was an eerie feeling, standing and overlooking the Valley of Megiddo, where the Battle of Armageddon will be fought when Jesus returns to the earth at His Second Coming. There are just too many other places and experiences to mention.

After we left Israel, we went to Athens, Greece where the airlines finally recognized that Gretnia's luggage was not going to catch up with us. The airlines took Gretnia and let her pick out a complete new outfit, from top to bottom and a new pair of shoes as well. I can tell you, Gretnia was excited! Brother Scott had been to Athens a number of times before and knew a furrier who sold many of us beautiful fur coats. I paid $80 for Gretnia's mink jacket. When we got home, I had it appraised, and it appraised for $400. That wasn't such a bad deal!

Our last stop was in Rome, Italy. We visited the place where Paul had been kept in prison. It does something to you when you realize what Paul had to endure before his death. We visited the Coliseum where the Christians were martyred. It makes you thankful that we live today and not then!

As wonderful as I thought the Holy Land trip was I had no idea then what else the Lord had in store for Gretnia and me. Our journey of faith was about to take another giant step.

After the first of the year in 1969, Brother Scott announced that he was going to retire on Easter Sunday. The church board asked if I would be interested in becoming pastor. They informed me that if I would be interested, they wanted to have the church vote on us before they considered any other candidates. That absolutely blew my mind! I couldn't conceive that they really wanted me to allow my name to be run for pastor. After all, I was only 31 at the time and Faith Tabernacle was one of the greatest churches in Oklahoma. Faith was our home church. Faith was where I received my start in the ministry. Gretnia and I were married there. Our children had been dedicated there.

There was something that clicked in my heart when the board asked me if they could run my name. I felt that, that is what the Lord's will was for our lives, so I told them I would be honored for them to do so.

I will never forget that Sunday morning, March 9, 1969. Brother Scott had scheduled the vote for after the morning service. Gretnia and I could hardly breathe as we waited for the board to count the ballots. I watched Brother Harvey Imke, who was the secretary of the board, as he came down the stairs, to see if I could tell anything from the expression on his face. He just had a somber look, so I couldn't tell anything. He gave the report of the ballot to Brother Scott. Brother Scott told the congregation that Gretnia and I had received 91% of the vote, and had been elected pastors of Faith Tabernacle! I could hardly believe it! We had been voted in as pastors of our home church! Our journey of faith had just taken another giant step!

Then Brother Scott told the congregation the story of what he had experienced earlier. He said that about a year or so before, he had come out of his office where he had been praying, and had come into the sanctuary. When he came into the sanctuary, he saw me working on the platform, putting up birch paneling. My father-in-law, Tommy Grant, had asked me to come and help install the paneling, even though I was pastor in El Reno at the time. He was short-handed and wanted to get the remodeling of the church done as quickly as possible, so I had agreed to come and help.

Brother Scott told the church that when he saw me working on the church that day in the sanctuary, the Lord had spoken to his heart and told him that I would be the next pastor, because it was evident that I had a great love for the church. Brother Scott had never told anyone about that experience until after the vote was taken. It was evident that he had not tried to influence the vote.

What was happening was beyond my comprehension. If I had gone to the church in Duncan earlier in our ministry, I would not have been available for Faith Tabernacle. It was evident the Lord was leading our lives. The timing of the Lord is such an important thing in our lives. We can miss the perfect will of God if we do not spend a great deal of time in prayer, seeking the perfect will of the Lord! It had been a step of faith to turn down the church in Duncan and to stay in El Reno, but the Lord had been leading our lives.

Brother Scott talked to me a great deal before he left the church. He wanted me to know some things he felt would help me in the transition from their ministry to our ministry. He told me that I should not be alarmed if people left after he and Sister Scott left the church. He told me that every shepherd gets his own sheep. If people left the church, it would not be because they did not love Gretnia and me, but that we were not their shepherds. He told me that he never went after people when they left because he knew that he was not their shepherd. If he had been their shepherd, then they would not have left. That became my philosophy in our ministry.

Brother Scott called me into his office one day and told me he had something he wanted to give me. He showed me his entire library and told me he had read every book in it. He told me how important it was to have adequate reading materials in the ministry. Then he said, "Kenneth, I want you to have all of my books for your ministry!" He gave me his entire library with the exception of a few books that he wanted for his own pleasure! There were eight complete sets of commentaries and numerous other study books. There was no way to put a value on what he had given me because there were so many out of print books included in his library. He had given me just what I needed to help prepare my messages. There was no way to adequately thank him for what he had done.

Easter Sunday morning, April 6, 1969 was Brother and Sister Scott's last service. There were 501 in attendance. The church gave them a beautiful 1969 Chevrolet station wagon that morning. It was just a small token of gratitude for all their years of service. They had become pastors in March of 1951. The church had made great strides during their years of ministry. The church had been down in attendance and had been struggling when they became pastors. They left a strong church in every way. It was one of the largest, if not the largest in attendance, in the district. It was at the top in missions giving. The church was blessed and had a wonderful reputation of giving beautiful Christmas pageants in the Civic Center Music Hall in downtown Oklahoma City. The church had been truly blessed under their leadership. Now it was up to Gretnia and me to carry on the great work the Scotts had begun. It would take a lot more faith to get the job done.

It was exciting assuming the responsibility of being pastor of Faith Tabernacle. My faith in the Lord had brought me that far, but little did I realize how much more my faith was going to be tested in the years that were ahead, and how much more my faith was going to grow.

In our first service, Sunday night April 6, 1969, three were saved and four were filled with the Holy Spirit and three joined the church. We were off and running for the Lord! I had the choir, in that first service, to march in singing, "A Highway to Heaven." There was a wonderful move of the Holy Spirit.

Faith Tabernacle was considerably larger than El Reno, but El Reno gave us more money than we received at Faith. Brother Scott had taken the church when it was in trouble and his agreement with the board was that he would receive a percentage of the offerings and they would not know how much he received. That had been the case all the years he had been pastor. When he resigned, the board found out how much he had been getting, and decided to place me on a salary, instead of a percentage like he had been receiving. So, I was in a bigger church, with a greater responsibility, yet receiving less money. I have stated earlier in my book that I never allowed what I was going to receive as my remuneration to affect me in accepting a church. The most important thing was, that I knew it was the will of the Lord to be there, and that He would supply all of our needs. Money is not the most important thing in life, but the perfect will of the Lord is!

The rest of the year was exciting for Gretnia and me. We were beginning to feel more and more at home. There were some who left the church after Brother and Sister Scott left. Some were people who we knew well, and who had been close friends with Gretnia's family. What Brother Scott had told me about every shepherd getting his own sheep though was a great help to me. I told them when they left that the door was always open to them if they ever wanted to return. What Gretnia and I noticed, however, was that there were a lot of new people coming who were closer to our age.

We held a Vacation Bible School that June with an average of 230 each night. Jerry B. Walker came in August for special services and we had a Missions Convention in September with Rev. Bennie and Colleen Tipton. The Lord was moving and blessing the church.

As we approached the beginning of a New Year, I began feeling two great needs in the church. First of all, I was longing for the Lord to give us a mighty, Holy Ghost revival like the church had had in its early days. I was reminded of the Aimee Semple McPherson revival in June of 1928, when Faith Tabernacle had dirt floors and seated 2000. Sister McPherson had five services a day. The police department of Oklahoma City controlled the crowds by allowing 2000 at a time to enter the church. When one service was over, they would allow 2000 more into the church. This was done five times a day for two weeks in the month of June. The church had no air conditioning at the time and it was reported that the temperature reached 110 during the crusade, but still, the people came. It was stated that there were as many as 10,000 people on the outside of the church waiting to get into the services. I have the complete report in the August,

1928, edition of the "Bridal Call Magazine," produced by Aimee Semple McPherson, in an article entitled, "The Great Southwest Revival."

Smith Wigglesworth, Charles S. Price, and Raymond T. Richey had also conducted revivals in Faith Tabernacle. There had been tremendous days of revival during the history of Faith Tabernacle, but I wanted to see it happen again.

I'll never forget what the Lord spoke to my heart as I prayed for Him to "Do it again!" He asked me if I were willing to pay the same price for revival that the early-day pastors had paid. He reminded me that there was a price to pay for revival because revivals do not come easily. He told me that if I were willing to fast, pray, and seek His face diligently, that He would send an old-fashioned, Holy Ghost revival.

I believe with all of my heart that that is the reason we are not seeing revival in our churches today. We live in the **"micro-wave age"** where we want the very best that the Lord has to offer, but we want it on our terms. We have **"revivalettes for Christianettes!"** We do not allow Him the needed time to give us a Holy Ghost revival. We try to limit our special services to a Sunday or maybe a Sunday through Wednesday. It takes time for the Holy Spirit to move and bring conviction to our hearts. We cannot rush the Holy Spirit into doing it on our terms. We are not to use the Holy Spirit; He is to use us!

I began the first of the year in 1970 preaching about revival. I called on the church to fast and pray. We began men's prayer meetings at 6:00 A.M., Monday through Friday. I called on the church to spend at least one day a week in fasting. We began the necessary preparation for the Lord to create a hunger in our hearts for revival. You see, it is always up to us to do our part, because the Lord will always do His part. If His Word is going to produce a harvest, it must fall on prepared and fertile soil. What is stated in **2 Chronicles 7:14** is true, **"If my people, which are called by my name, shall humble themselves, and pray, and seek my face, and turn from their wicked ways;**

then will I hear from heaven, and will forgive their sin, and will heal their land."

The second need I felt for the church was the need of a full-size gymnasium. If we were going to be able to take care of the growth we were experiencing in our youth; we needed a place for them. We had hired a fine young couple, Steve and Vada Allen, who had come to us from the Tennessee District to be our youth pastors. I had known Steve and Vada when they traveled as evangelists, knew they were greatly anointed by the Holy Spirit, and felt that they would be a great asset to us. Indeed, they were! They were not with us very long, however, because the Lord opened the door for them to pastor a church in Kansas.

The Lord enabled us to construct a beautiful, full-size gymnasium, complete with a kitchen, dressing rooms for men and women, and restrooms. Our youth had a regular meeting place in the new gym called the "Upper Room," which was located above all the other rooms on the East end of the building. The gym proved to be a tremendous blessing to the church because it was used every week. We were able to have our church dinners there as well as use it for all of our basketball teams. Our gym had become the second gym in the city built by an Assembly of God church. And, Praise the Lord, we were able to pay cash for the gym as we built it, even though it took all of our extra cash to do so.

We were still having our men's prayer meeting after the gym had been built. It was after one of the prayer meetings, that George Bell's car would not start. George was one of the men in our church whom I had known for quite some time. I pulled my car along side George's car so I could attach jumper cables, in an attempt to get his car started. I told George not to attempt to start his car until I had the cables attached to the battery posts. As I was bending over the battery, attaching the cable to the positive post on George's car, he turned the ignition on in an attempt to start his car. When he turned the ignition on, the battery exploded in my face!

The concussion was so great that it lifted my body off the ground and threw me onto my car. My face was burning and blood was pouring out of the wounds between my eyes. I ran into the kitchen of the gym and began washing my face with water. I could not see out of my left eye. I simply thought that I had blood in my eye. I took the contact lenses out of my eyes, hoping that would help. It did not help. I still could not see out of my left eye. The men took me to St. Anthony's hospital where they sewed up the wounds between my eyes and then they called for Dr. William A. Cunningham, my ophthalmologist, who came and examined my eyes. He told me that my left eye had sustained considerable damage, but that he could not tell about the inside of my eye because it was filled with blood. I asked him when I would be able to see again. He paused for a moment, and then said, "It could be three months, or six months, or . . . maybe never." It all depends on how healthy your eye is." He then admitted me into the hospital after he had put patches over both eyes, and left instructions for me to sit up in my bed at all times.

I'll never forget when my mother came into the room to see me for the first time. She began screaming, "Oh no, he's blind, he's blind!" We quickly explained to her that I just had patches over my eyes to protect them.

Early the next morning, Dr. Cunningham came by to see how I was doing. He removed the patch from my left eye, and was starting to remove the patch from my right eye, when I cried, "Dr. Cunningham, I can see, I can see!" He said, "You can't. It's impossible!" I said, "I don't know if it is possible or not, but I can see Harold Price standing at the foot of my bed." Harold, who was one of my deacons, had come by to see how I was doing. I could see him clearly! Dr. Cunningham never did remove the patch from my right eye that morning.

Dr. Cunningham called for a nurse and asked her to bring

him the necessary equipment so he could examine my eye. After he had checked my left eye, he told me that all of the blood was gone from the inside of my eye, and all he could see was a small scar where my eye had been injured. I asked him what he was going to write on my medical chart about my eye. He told me that he was going to say a miracle had occurred: that I had experienced a phenomenon! I knew that I had experienced a miracle! I knew that the Lord had answered my prayer and the prayers of so many people! My faith was growing by leaps and bounds!

Around this time, the Lord sent us another wonderful couple, Dean and Peggy Galyen. They were hired as Youth Pastors and Ministers of Music. I had actually contacted Peggy's brother to see if he was interested in the job, and he gave me Dean and Peggy's names. They proved to be a great blessing. Dean worked with the choir and music as well as the youth. It was during his tenure that Faith developed an outstanding Bible Quiz team. Our young people, under his direction, also did extremely well in Teen Talent competition. Our Bible Quiz team won the district competition three years in a row under Dean's leadership. As a reward for their winning we took them to Dallas to eat at our favorite place, "Southern Kitchen Restaurant." We had an exciting competition to see who could eat the most boiled shrimp there.

I felt impressed to contact Jerry B. Walker about coming for revival, beginning the first Sunday of January 1971. He had been with Brother Scott twice and had been with us for a Sunday in 1969. I scheduled the services for two weeks beginning January 3rd. I put an ad in the Daily Oklahoman the Saturday before the revival began to announce the beginning of the revival.

We began the special services on the scheduled date and went through the first week and through Thursday night the second week without any thing special happening. At the end of that second Thursday night service, I told the people I felt the Lord was trying to move, but that we needed to do something more for that to happen. I asked everyone who could, to fast with me the next day. There were many who joined with me and fasted all day Friday.

Friday evening, just before the service began, an ambulance pulled up in front of the church. I went to see why the ambulance was there, just as they were unloading an eighteen-year-old young man. He told me that he lived in Chandler, Oklahoma, which was about sixty-miles from the church. He told me he had a condition which had caused the deterioration of his bones, and, that his bones could no longer support his weight if he tried to walk. As a result of his condition, he was confined to bed for the rest of his life.

I asked why he had come to the church that night. He told me that he had seen the ad in the newspaper that announced we would be praying for the sick each night. He told me he had followed my ministry and knew that many had been healed in my revivals, and that as he was praying that week, he felt impressed to ask his folks to bring him to the revival so we could pray for his healing.

We took him into the church and placed him at the end of the altar area on his stretcher. He stayed there until Jerry B. had finished his message and had given the invitation. Then Jerry B. and I went over, laid our hands on him, and prayed, asking the Lord to heal him.

The best way to describe what happened is: he screamed like a Cherokee Indian, leaped off the stretcher, landed on his feet, and began leaping and running, up and down the aisle, speaking in tongues, baptized in the Holy Ghost, instantly healed by the power of the Lord!

The word of his healing spread like wild fire. The church was full on Sunday, and we continued the revival the third week. It seemed as though the floodgates of heaven were opened. Miracles began occurring each night. The church was filling, night after night, as the Lord moved mightily. By the fourth week, our church couldn't hold the crowd. Faith Tabernacle normally seated 640. There were four sections of pews with sixteen rows in each section. The normal seating for each row was ten people.

By the fourth week we had to unbolt all of the pews and move them forward, so that we could put in the 360 folding chairs we had rented. People were coming as early as 1:00 P.M. to hold seats for the service, which did not begin until 7:30 P.M. It became necessary to keep the church locked until 5:00 P.M., at which time we allowed people to come in. We would not let them hold seats for anyone. As soon as we opened the doors, people would rush in to get the front row seats. They wanted to be able to see the many miracles that were happening. It seems that today, people get to church early in order to get the back seats!

Even though it was in the middle of the winter, we had to turn on the air conditioning because of the body heat of so many people. The church had outside water towers to operate our air conditioning, and it was so cold that the towers would freeze, preventing us from using our air conditioning. As a result, while the revival was going on, we had to change our system over to central air and heat.

Even though we had seating for 1000 people with the addition of the 360 folding chairs, the church still would not hold the crowds as the revival continued. We had a youth chapel immediately adjacent to the sanctuary, which seated 250. We set up closed circuit TV in that room with a huge 12' by 12' screen. That room filled quickly each night, so we started using the platform in the main sanctuary to allow seating for our choir. I have pictures taken during the revival, of over 1500 people a night crowding into the church. People had to stand all around the church to be in the services.

People came with every kind of need imaginable. Blinded eyes were opened, deaf ears were unstopped. One night a lady with a huge goiter came forward for healing. When Jerry B. laid his hands on her, immediately, in front of everyone, the goiter disappeared!

The media, with representatives from the TV stations and the daily newspaper, came night after night. We did reserve seats for them because they were reporting about the revival. Jerry B. and I were guests on live TV programs, talking about the revival. The newspaper carried stories, reporting about the miracles and the crowds in the services.

There were nights when the visible glory of the Lord settled like a cloud in the sanctuary. There were nights when you could hear angels singing. As I have traveled over the state of Oklahoma, I have had people come to me and tell about the night they were in the revival in 1971 and heard the angels singing. I have had others tell me they were saved or filled with the Holy Spirit in the revival. The revival impacted the entire state!

One night a lady who had been blind since birth came across the platform for prayer. When Jerry B. prayed for her she screamed, "I can see, I can see!" He asked if she could see the clock on the back wall. Then he asked if she could tell us the time. She told us the time because she could see the clock clearly. She rejoiced in seeing her family for the first time. It was a time of great rejoicing. However, as she walked off the platform, fear gripped her heart, she became afraid that she would lose her sight, and, just as suddenly as she had received her sight, she lost it. The devil literally robbed her of her sight because she became fearful that she would lose it. It was just as Job had stated in **Job 3:25, "For the thing which I greatly feared is come upon me, and that which I was afraid of is come unto me."**

It became necessary to have a number of our men to act as "catchers." So many people were falling prostrate under the power of God, that I didn't want anyone to fall and claim to have hurt themselves. I have always preached and told people, that if the power of the Lord is really upon you, you will fall and never be hurt, but if you fall in the flesh, you can injure yourself. I wanted to protect those who may have fallen in the flesh.

I cancelled all of our basketball games because of the revival. We had won the championship in the city's open league the year before, so we had a tremendous team, but our revival was more important than ball games. I cancelled Royal Rangers and Missionettes. I brought all of the children above the age of three into the services. I wanted them to experience the outpouring of the Holy Spirit. They witnessed things they have never forgotten.

What a revival! By actual count of those who gave us their names and addresses, there were more than 3000 saved and more than 1500 filled with the Holy Spirit. The miracles were too numerous to count. Many who came to the revival in casts, braces, and wheelchairs, left healed by the power of God. The gifts of the Spirit operated in the services. I would stand amazed, as people I knew would come through the line and Jerry B. would tell them what their needs were before they could tell him. It was an experience I will never forget. The Lord had answered my prayer for revival. We had started the first Sunday of January, and closed on Easter Sunday, April 11. We had experienced fourteen weeks of heaven on earth!

There were a number of things that amazed me about the revival. Even though we had services Sunday through Friday each week for fourteen weeks, when the meeting was over, the scholastic achievement in school, for all of our children and youth, had improved. The tithes and offerings tripled from what they had been before the meeting began. Our attendance had doubled. We had experienced a sovereign move of the Holy Spirit that changed our church. If you want to see how much your church has benefited from a revival, look at the results achieved from the meeting. Ask yourself, "Does the fruit remain?"

As I look back to the meeting, I have one regret. I believe it would have been better if we had not closed the revival when we did. The revival should have continued! Jerry B. and I have discussed that fact a number of times. It is a subject upon which we both agree. I know one thing; my faith level had increased considerably. The Lord had shown me that He is faithful, if we are faithful to Him. The Lord had shown me, that if we fast and pray and seek His face, that He would give us the desires of our hearts. The Lord had given us a mighty outpouring of His Holy Spirit, just as He had done in the early days of Faith Tabernacle.

After the revival, we had to move the pews back into place, which reduced the seating in the sanctuary back to the original seating capacity. However, the pews were now full, and that had not been the case before the revival.

We rejoiced to see the many new people coming to the church after the revival. As I stated previously, we had doubled in attendance. It was exciting getting them plugged into the church. The Holy Spirit impacted our worship services. We had always had good services, but after the revival, there was a greater liberty in worshipping the Lord.

I don't know if it was because of the revival or not, but I received an invitation to preach the Pleasant Grove camp meeting, of the Peninsular District of the Assemblies of God, in Plant City, Florida later that year. I knew that word had spread all over the country about the revival at Faith Tabernacle, and I received a number of invitations to speak at special events. The camp meeting was a wonderful experience for me. It lasted ten days. All heaven came down the very first night as a minister from the area, who had rheumatoid arthritis, was instantly healed, and began dancing in the Spirit across the front of the tabernacle. There were many more miracles of healing in the camp meeting as well. I had the privilege of being teamed with Cy Homer, the president at that time, of Southeastern Assemblies of God College. Brother Homer was the morning Bible teacher for the camp meeting. He was an outstanding preacher of the Gospel. I will never forget the dynamic sermon series he preached, entitled, "Thou That Leadest Joseph Like a Flock."

1972 proved to be an exciting year as well. One of the greatest miracles I have ever seen happened in one of our Sunday morning services. I had been seated on the platform when I looked up and saw one of our men, Jewell Armstrong, leading a black man into the service. I noticed that he had a red-tipped cane hanging over his arm, indicating he was blind. When they arrived at their seat, Brother Armstrong handed a note to one of the ushers, asking him to give the note to me. When I read the note, Brother Armstrong had asked me to be sure and pray for the sick that morning, because he had brought his friend who needed healing.

When I received the note, I announced to the church that I would be praying for the sick at the end of the service. After my message, I invited those who needed healing to come forward for prayer. A number of people responded. As they began coming forward for prayer, I lined them up across the front of the church. The black man wound up in the center aisle of the church. I did not pray for the blind man first. Instead, I went to the end of the line and started praying for the people. The Lord began touching people immediately.

Finally, I came to the black man, and asked him his name. He told me his name was Johnny Jones. I asked him his age. He told me he was 72. I asked him how long he had been blind. He told me he had been blind for 36 years. I asked him what had caused his blindness. He told me he had been working with an acetylene torch and somehow it had slipped in his hand. When it slipped, the flame had cut across his eyes, blinding him. I asked him if anything could ever be done to enable him to see again. He told me that the doctors had told him there was nothing that could be done to restore his sight. I asked him why he had come to Faith Tabernacle that morning. He informed me that he was Baptist, and that he had never been in a Pentecostal church before, but that he was praying that week and the Lord had impressed upon his heart to call his friend, Jewell Armstrong, to see if it would be all right for him to come to church for prayer. Jewell had assured him it would be all right. I asked him if he really believed that the Lord could heal him. He said, "That's the reason I am here!"

I asked the church to join with me as we prayed for

Johnny. I prayed fervently. I quoted Scriptures. I then asked Johnny if he could see. He tried to blink his eyes, but he couldn't see. I prayed again. I prayed louder. I quoted more Scriptures. I asked him again if he could see. Again, he tried to blink his eyes, but to no avail. He still couldn't see. The devil came and told me I was making a fool of myself. The devil told me I didn't have the faith for Johnny to be healed. That is when you need boldness in the Lord! I informed the devil that I was not the healer. Jesus is the healer! It was my responsibility to lay hands on the sick and pray, but the Lord would do the healing. I told Johnny that we had prayed twice: once, in the name of the Father, and the second time, in the name of His Son, Jesus. Then I told him that we were going to pray in the name of the Holy Spirit, the third person of the Godhead.

I then asked the congregation to put their hands over their eyes, as a point of contact, as they joined with me to pray for Johnny. When I began praying, I realized that I was praying in tongues. The words flowed like a river. I listened as the congregation was praying. It sounded like everyone was praying in the Holy Spirit. It sounded like waves washing upon the sands of the beach. It was beautiful. When I finished praying, I changed the question I had been asking. Instead of asking Johnny if he could see, I asked him if he could see any light. I'll never forget his answer as long as I live. He guided his hands and placed them on my shoulders and cried, **"Light? I see you!"** And, just like that, the Lord healed Johnny Jones! I don't have to tell you, but we had camp meeting that morning in Faith Tabernacle. People were rejoicing and praising the Lord for the mighty miracle we had witnessed. Our children and young people have never forgotten the creative miracle that the Lord performed that day. His story was told later in the book, "The History of Faith Tabernacle." Before Johnny left that day, he asked if I would stay at the church until he got home. I did not know at the time what his reason was.

Can you imagine what his wife thought when he walked

out to his car that day? She had dropped him off that morning because she didn't want to go into that Pentecostal church. Johnny saw the color of his car for the first time. He saw his wife for the first time in 36 years. As he approached the car, she asked why no one was helping him. Johnny said, "I don't need any help. The Lord has healed me and I can see!"

Just a little while later, I received his call at the church. Johnny told me on the phone that day that it had been 36 years since he had been able to read his Bible and he just wanted to see if he could still read it. Then he began reading the **23rd Psalm, "The Lord is my shepherd . . ."** We followed Johnny Jones for the next several years until he died in his eighties. He retained his sight until he died! That experience was another tremendous boost in my faith.

As we had entered into the New Year, it became apparent that I needed additional staff to help take care of the growth we had experienced through the revival. I scheduled several interviews at Southwestern Assemblies of God University in Waxahachie, Texas. After I had interviewed several of the candidates, I met another young man by the name of Jimmie L. McNabb. He had not been on the list of candidates, but had been invited by a friend of his, Jerry Elder, whom I had scheduled for an interview, to come with him. After I had talked with Jerry and he started to leave, Jim had gotten up and started to leave with Jerry. I asked Jim if he would like to talk to me about the position, and he agreed to do so. After the interview, I felt impressed to ask him and his wife Linda, to come to Faith Tabernacle as our new associate pastors. That decision proved to be divinely ordered by the Lord. It is amazing how the Lord works. **Psalms 37:23** states **"The steps of a good man are ordered by the Lord; and he delighteth in his way. "** Jim became our Christian Educational Director. He told me later that he had at least read a book on the subject. He and Linda became great assets to the church, later becoming our Youth Pastors. They were with us for four years. Today he is the pastor of "The Bridge," formally,

Mustang Assembly of God, one of the great churches in the state. He is also the Assistant Superintendent of the Oklahoma District. The Lord certainly had a hand in bringing the McNabbs to Oklahoma.

It has often been stated that a church cannot hold the congregation, if it consistently runs in attendance, more than eighty percent capacity of the church. That was proving to be the case for us, because we were averaging more than the church would seat, and we were beginning to lose some people. You must have a plan for something new if you want the people to stay with you, therefore I began praying and asking the Lord what He wanted us to do.

I initially started looking for the property around the church. I felt that if we could purchase enough of the houses, that we could tear them all down, and have enough property to build the new sanctuary right where we were. That had been the dream of Brother Scott. I started walking around all the houses close to the church in that entire city block, claiming the property for the Lord. However, we were only able to purchase one house. The owners of the other houses would not sell them to us. A labor union owned the property at the end of the block, but they would not sell to us. I was running into a dead-end road every way that I turned.

As we began a New Year, I was voted in as president of the Assemblies of God Ministerial Alliance in Oklahoma City. The alliance began discussing starting an Assemblies of God school. During the time we were looking for property for the school, I found 28.04 acres located at I-40 and Portland Avenue. It was a wheat field, but would be a perfect location for what we wanted. When the alliance decided against starting the school, I felt so impressed to see if the church wanted to buy the land and build a new church on the property. The land was in a trust at one of the large banks in downtown Oklahoma City. I began getting all of the information I could about the property so I could present it to the board and the church.

When I presented my findings to the board and the church, on September 9, 1973 we voted to purchase the land for $336,720. We gave a $5000 check for the earnest money and had sixty days in which to raise an additional $60,000, which would be the down payment on the land. The balance of the money for the land was to be paid in four equal payments out of the sale of a bond program the church was doing to finance the building. I shared the need with the people, asking them to give sacrificially to raise the money. We came to the end of the sixty days and the money was not there. Word had come to us that there were several offers, larger than our offer, for the land. If we did not have the $60,000, we would lose the $5000 earnest money, and the sale would not go through, thus, causing us to lose the property.

I went into my study and fell on my face, at the same place I had prayed in the beginning, when I had asked the Lord if it were His will that we buy the property and build a new church. He had given me an assurance that He would be with us and would supply our every need if I would trust and obey Him. While I was praying, on the sixtieth day, the phone rang. It was my secretary, telling me I had a phone call from an attorney who wanted me to come to his office, which was only two blocks from the church. I drove to his office, where he introduced me to a gentleman from Houston, Texas. The attorney informed me that the man had insisted that I come to meet him **that** day. He then told me that the man's grandmother, who had attended Faith Tabernacle, had passed away and had left the church **$60,000.** That was the exact amount we needed to get the property! I took the money to the bank, wrote the check, and took it to the real estate company, securing the property. The Lord had done the miraculous. My faith had been tested! But, Praise the Lord, God had proven Himself again. My faith was soaring! The Lord was with us in our building program!

Isaiah 12:3 says **"Behold, God is my salvation (the word salvation here means: victory); I will trust, and not be afraid: for the Lord Jehovah is my strength and my song; he**

also is become my salvation (victory)." Psalms 56:3–4 says
**"What time I am afraid, I will trust in thee. In God I will
praise his word, in God I have put my trust . . ."** These two
portions of Scripture are very meaningful. They state that you
can trust and not be afraid or you can be afraid and still trust.
Either way, the Lord will see you through! The Lord had seen
us through!

We now had the property, but there was another problem. The property was zoned "I" meaning "Light Industrial."
We discovered that that was the only zoning in Oklahoma City
in which a church could not be built. When we had started nego-
tiations for the property, we had been told that it had been zoned
"A," which was "Agricultural," but that the property had been
changed to "I" in order for it to be sold as commercial property. The real estate company had told us they didn't think there
would be a problem in getting the zoning changed back to the
original zoning, however, since the property was a wheat field.
We had proceeded with that assumption. It turned out that that
was not the case.

When I went to the Oklahoma City Planning Commission to make application for a zoning change, I was told by the
director that he would see to it that we never built a church in
that location. I looked at him and said, "I don't know what your
belief in the Lord may be, but if the Lord wants us to build a
church at that location, you, nor anyone else, will stop us!" I can
understand why they would not want us to build a church there,
because it would have taken more than twenty-eight acres off of
their tax roll. About a month later, he was no longer on the job,
because he had been dismissed. However, that did not stop the
city from trying to keep us from changing the zoning.

All during this time we were working on the plans for
the new church. Gretnia and I had been going around the country, getting ideas about the type of building that we wanted to
build. I had told the church board in the beginning that the Lord
had shown me the colors that were to be used in the church.

The Lord had impressed **Revelation 4:3** upon my heart which says **"And he that sat was to look upon like a jasper and a sardine stone: and there was a rainbow round about the throne,** *in sight like unto an emerald.***"** I just knew that the Lord wanted our church colors to be emerald green, white, and gold. We would not need to have committees to decide about the color of the carpet, or the pews, or things of that nature. I have seen churches split over those kinds of decisions; however, I would not encourage anyone to do what I did, unless you have heard directly from the Lord about doing so.

We eventually had to go to court, because the city would not give us the zoning change. The judge ruled in our favor and instructed the city to give us the needed zoning change. He was very vocal in his remarks to the city, telling them that they had caused undo hardship on the church. Then he told them that they had thirty days in which to file an appeal, but that if they did file an appeal, they were to inform us by certified mail of their decision to do so.

I was scheduled to go to Lausanne, Switzerland for the International Congress on Evangelization, July 14, 1974, just before the thirty days were set to expire. I had a man for whom I had worked when I was a young man in Healdton, offer to pay my trip to the Congress if I would come to their church and give a report about the Congress. When I returned, I went to the First Methodist Church in my hometown, where I had gone to church the last two years I was in high school, and gave the report. While I was on the trip, I kept calling back to see if the church had received a letter from the city. I was told each time that we had not received a letter from them.

I arrived back from Switzerland about midnight on a Monday. I had been traveling about twenty-five hours when we landed back in Oklahoma City. I awakened about 6:00 A.M. Tuesday, unable to sleep. I got the Daily Oklahoman and started reading the newspaper. On page eight, at the bottom of the page, was an article stating that the city's attorney would be recommending to the City Council that morning that they file an appeal against Faith Tabernacle.

I quickly dressed and drove down to City Hall where the City Council was meeting at 8:00 A.M. that morning. I went to the mayor's office to see the mayor's secretary, who, along with her husband, had been attending Faith Tabernacle, and asked if I could speak in the council meeting. She told me that the agenda had already been set, but that I could have three minutes to speak as a citizen's privilege.

I waited until the agenda had been completed, and then they called my name to address the council. I told them why I was there. I told them that the judge had told the city to inform us, by certified mail, if they were going to appeal his decision, and that they had not done so. I told them about the trouble with the Planning Commission in trying to get the zoning changed for the property we had purchased. I told them we had the plans completed for the church and were ready to start construction if they would give us the zoning change. The city council members then called for the Planning Commission to bring the plans down for them to see what we were planning on building. By that time, I had been before the council for twenty minutes.

All of a sudden, a white-haired, older gentleman, who was seated on the front row, stood to his feet and said to the council, "I think it is time to let the church start building their building to worship the Lord, and it is time for the council to get on with the business of running the city!" Then he sat down. Immediately, one of the council members made a motion that the city not file the appeal, and, let Faith Tabernacle get started building it's building. The motion was immediately seconded, and the mayor called for the vote. Every council member hit their lights to vote. The vote was unanimous to let us start building!

I turned to find the older man who had addressed the council, **but he was not there.** I asked a number of people who were in the council chamber, if they knew who he was. **No one**

had ever seen him before! I asked the mayor's secretary if she knew who he was. She told me that she had never seen him before. I went back a number of times to see if I could find him. I never saw him again. **There is not a doubt in my mind that the Lord sent an angel to help us get our church built!** What do you think that did for my faith? Faith can move mountains! **A huge mountain had just been moved! We serve a miracle-working God! Two great miracles had already occurred in our building program! Miracles build faith!**

The church body voted to enter into a $1,000,000 bond program in order to finance the building of the new church. The estimated cost of the new church complex, which would seat 2000 in worship, complete with educational facilities and a full-size gymnasium, was $1,600,000. A group of men from a local union met in our old church and voted unanimously to purchase the facilities for $600,000. We had received pledges for an additional $60,000 from people within the church. We felt we had the plan to pay for our new church.

We kicked off the bond sale in November 1974. We had been told that as soon as we had sold enough bonds, we could start construction! We had groundbreaking ceremonies on the new property in January 1975. Construction on the 72,000 square feet facility actually began in April 1975. What an exciting day!

I had always wanted to have Bill Hedrick, who had been the piano player and arranger for the Sentries quartet, to be with me as our Minister of Music. I was blessed to have him and his wife Vera, with us, serving in that capacity. Bill played the piano and Scott Taylor, who had been the lead singer in the Sentries, began leading our worship full time. The Lord had given me a desire of my heart. Those were special times in our lives!

We had started a revival with Don and Neta Brankel on March 23 that year that lasted until May 4. Just think—a seven-week revival! That is unheard of today! Forty-seven people were saved and fifty-two were filled with the Holy Spirit.

Brother Brankel was with us every year for revival. Later that year, he and Sister Brankel went with us to the Holy Land. I also took Bill and Vera Hedrick with us on that Holy Land trip. In fact, in 1973 I had taken Dean and Peggy Galyen with me to the Holy Land, and in 1974 I had taken Jim and Linda McNabb. I had wanted my associates to experience the same wonderful joy that Gretnia and I had experienced when we had the privilege of going to the Holy Land.

We had a wet year in 1975. It took a long time to get the church off the ground. We had difficulty in getting the foundation and floor poured. There was a lot of plumbing and in-ground work that had to be done. As I mentioned earlier, the property we bought had been a wheat field. As a result, the ground was very susceptible to holding moisture in the ground. The property was literally a quagmire.

The church was built with double masonry construction. We had brick on the outside of the wall and concrete blocks on the inside of the wall. We also put steel in the walls and poured concrete into the walls, forming pilasters, which would enable us to support a second floor if it were ever needed. By this time we were well into the year of 1976. The walls were being built. It was so exciting to see progress on the building.

I felt it was important for us to keep up the excitement about the new church being built, even though we were experiencing delays in getting it built. We decided to take the church body to the new location and have a Sunday morning service there. We did not have the steel for the roof and all we had were walls around us, but we had a wonderful service as the choir sang, "We've Come This Far by Faith." We also had workdays, when the church would go out to the new location, and clean up around the area. It was a great time of fellowship for us as well.

When we placed the order for the steel, we were told that there would be a long delay, because the nation was having a shortage of steel, but that we could have the steel for the south wing of the educational facility, as well as the steel for the gymnasium, by the first part of 1977. We were told that the heavy structural steel for the sanctuary would not be available until the following year.

We decided to finish the part of the church for which we could get the steel. There would be plenty of restrooms, a kitchen, and an area for the youth above the kitchen, a place to worship, and a place to have Sunday School.

I had been praying in the first part of 1977 about whom the Lord would have me to invite for special services. I could not get away from inviting Mike Warnke, former Satanist high priest. I had never seen him nor had I heard him speak, but I felt the Lord wanted me to have him come to Faith Tabernacle. I called and made the arrangements for him to be with us on February 5th and 6th of that year.

I was not prepared for what I encountered when I saw him get off the plane. He was wearing a black leather outfit, had yellow lenses in his glasses, and a long ponytail in his hair. I swallowed hard. I was pretty old-fashioned, to say the least, and I asked myself, "Are you sure this is what you want in the church?" We got into the car and started driving to the church. All he wanted to talk about was the Lord and what the Lord had done for him. We went into my office to pray before we went out for the service that Saturday evening. As we began praying, the Holy Spirit began moving, and all of us began praying in the Spirit. My fears vanished! Mike was with us that Saturday evening and all day Sunday. There were 57 saved in those services. The Lord had taught me the importance of listening closely to Him and being obedient to what He wanted. My ideas of whom the Lord could use were changing.

I was hopeful that we could have the new building finished in time for the General Council of the Assemblies of God, which was being held in Oklahoma City in August of 1977. We did not make it however.

I scheduled Dean Galyen, who had been our Minister of Music and Youth for four years; to speak on Wednesday night before the council started. I also had C. M. Ward and Don Brankel scheduled to speak on Sunday morning August 21, and the McDuff Brothers were to be with us for the Sunday evening service. We had to have the services in the old location because the new building was not ready. The old building was packed to capacity that Sunday.

The next Sunday, August 28th, was the last Sunday in the old church. I spoke that morning on the subject, "The History of Faith Tabernacle." Faith Tabernacle had had a wonderful history in that location. The church had been in the same location for fifty years. It was hard for some people to leave. In fact, when we moved, we lost about ten percent of the congregation. I tried to tell the people that the "church," was really the congregation, not the brick and mortar of the building; however, it was still hard for some to visualize that fact.

The following Sunday morning, September 4, 1977, the congregation met at the old location, 1110 N.W. 2nd, and went as a caravan to the new location, 800 S. Portland. We had purchased new folding chairs, which had been placed in the gym for seating. We had built a platform where the pulpit and musical instruments were placed. We arranged chairs for the choir on the platform. A sound system had been installed. I must admit, the sound was really alive! There was a lot of echoing because of the hard walls of the gym. We eventually had to put up panels of insulation on the walls and install carpet to deaden the sound. But, everything was ready for our arrival!

I don't know how the congregation must have felt when they moved from the small abandoned schoolhouse, where the church had started in 1925, in the neighborhood known as Mulligan Gardens, to the new church on N.W. 2nd, but we had a wonderful beginning in our new church that morning. Three were saved and two were filled with the Holy Spirit that first day. The Lord was there and the Holy Spirit moved in a mighty way! It was a great day in the history of Faith Tabernacle!

I'll never forget the comments of some people after we

moved into the gym. They said, "You can tell where the priorities of McGee are. He cares more about having a place to play and have fun, than he does about having a place to worship." They couldn't understand that if we had not gone ahead and taken the steel to build the gym and educational facilities that it would have been another year before we were able to meet in the new building at all because the heavy structural steel needed for the sanctuary would not be in till the following year. By taking the steel to build the gym and educational facilities, we were at least able to have some place to worship in our new location an entire year earlier than had we not taken the steel needed for those facilities.

By the time we had reached this place in building the church, we had spent all of the money from the bond program. It was time to complete the sale of the old church to the local union, which had voted unanimously to buy the church. When we contacted them about closing the sale, however, they informed us that they had changed their mind, and would not be taking the buildings. We were floored by their decision! We had not signed a contract with them because of who they were. We felt if we could trust anyone, we could trust them. However, that proved to be false.

That left us without the money to complete the new church! We began immediately trying to find another buyer for the old church. It was not an easy thing to do. There were not a lot of people looking to buy an old church. We did find two young ladies who wanted to have a children's ministry in the old facilities. It was better to have someone in the building, keeping it up, than to leave it empty.

I began looking for a place to secure a loan to finish the new church. Again, there were not a lot of places that were willing to loan money to a church that was only partially built. They had fears about the possibility of liens being filed on the uncompleted building. It became a long process, trying to find a loan. Several months rolled by without my finding a loan.

I will never forget the many times, while driving down Portland Avenue, that I prayed, "Lord, help us get a loan, so we can finish the building." I cried and prayed, day after day, for the Lord to open a door for us. It was heartbreaking to see the church sitting there, without any work being done on it.

Without realizing it, I began pushing the people, by preaching on "faith." It became so bad, that in one of our board meetings, one of our deacons, who was also one of my best friends, Scott Taylor, stood up and hit the table, and said, "Faith, faith, faith . . . I get so tired of hearing about faith."

It was not long after that, Bill Shell, another close friend and deacon, came to my office and told me he had been awakened that morning with a scripture on his heart for me. He asked me to turn to **James 3:14–17**. It says **"But if ye have bitter envying and strife in your hearts, glory not, and lie not against the truth. This wisdom descendeth not from above, but is earthly, sensual, devilish. For where envying, and strife is, there is confusion and every evil work. But the wisdom that is from above is first pure, then peaceable, gentle, and easy to be intreated, full of mercy and good fruits, without partiality, and without hypocrisy."** He then asked me, "Which wisdom have you been using in the church? Has your wisdom brought about envy and strife or peace and good fruits?" It was like I had been hit between the eyes with a bat! I had been pushing the people, instead of leading them; I had allowed envy and strife to come into the church.

I thanked Bill for coming by, and then immediately called Scott and asked if he could come by the church so that I could talk to him. He came to my office and I told him what Bill Shell had shared with me, and then I asked him to forgive me for pushing instead of leading. We embraced and had a good cry and he left. The Lord then spoke to my heart about what I had to do the following Sunday morning.

During my message the following Sunday morning, I shared with the congregation what had happened to me that week. I told them that I had apologized to Scott and that I wanted to apologize to them as well. I told them I had been pushing them instead of leading them, and that a good shepherd leads the sheep. I was not prepared for what happened next. People started standing, apologizing to me for the things they had been saying about me. It turned into a tremendous time of healing for the entire church. The Holy Spirit had brought about a tremendous miracle. The envy and strife disappeared. Things began running smoothly. I felt we were on course again.

In my search for a loan for the church, someone had mentioned a group called Service Investment Corporation. It was an organization that had access to every savings and loan association and bank in the state of Oklahoma. I contacted them and asked for an appointment with the president.

When I met with him, I told him that we needed a loan for $1,600,000. That would enable us to pay off the bonds and finish the church. He looked at me and told me that I must be dreaming. He informed me that it would be impossible to get a loan because of the possibility of liens being filed on the uncompleted building. I told him that I believed in miracles, and asked him if he would at least try to get us a loan. He told me not to hold my breath, but that he would try. He took all of the information, about the church and me, and told me he would do his best.

It was during this time that I heard people talking and saying, "If it were the Lord's will to build, then we would not be having this kind of trouble. Kenneth is just trying to build a monument to himself." That was awfully hard to take, but I knew that the Lord was with us in building the church. In fact, **Ezra 3:4–5** states, **"Then the people of the land weakened the hands of the people of Judah, and troubled them in building, And hired counselors against them, to frustrate their purpose, all the days of Cyrus king of Persia, even until the reign of Darius king of Persia."** I knew that the devil did not want us to build the new building and that he was doing everything he could to keep us from finishing the project.

I received a call one day from the president of Service Investment Corporation, asking me to come to his office. When I went in and sat down across the desk from where he was seated, he pushed a piece of paper towards me. He said, "Reverend, here is your miracle. This is your letter of commitment for $1,600,000." He then told me how it had come about. He said he had mailed the information about the church to all of the savings and loan associations and banks in the state. He said he received a call from the president of the Custer County Federal Savings and Loan Association in Weatherford, Oklahoma, asking if I were the same Kenneth McGee who had been pastor of the El Reno Assembly of God church. He told him that I was the same man. The man from Weatherford told him that if I were the same man, that he would participate to his maximum, which would be $400,000, and that, he had three friends who would also participate with their limit of $400,000 each. He then told him about the loan I had secured when I was pastor in El Reno. He said that I had never been late on my payments, (that I had in fact been a month ahead most of the time), and that if I had anything to do with the loan for Faith Tabernacle, he would participate. It pays to have a good record!

In order to get the loan, I had to have a number of people who were willing to put up their financial statements, and sign the papers for the loan. I began first with the board members, and then asked other people in the church if they would be willing to do so. I was thrilled with the response of the people. We pledged our support and signed the first set of papers to secure the loan. It would be necessary at a later date to renew our commitment and sign the final papers, securing the permanent loan. I was excited about what the Lord was doing.

As we drew close to time to commit our financial statements and sign the final papers to secure the loan, I began receiving phone calls from different board members saying that they would not be able to sign the papers. In order to release them, I had to find someone with as large of financial statement as theirs. I was able to do that, which greatly relieved me.

On Friday, before the Monday we were to sign the final papers and secure the loan, I received a phone call from another board member who told me he had talked it over with his wife and family, and that he could not sign the papers. He told me he was more liquid with his income, and felt that if we could not make the payments, which he didn't think we could make, they would come to him in order to get the money. I pleaded with him to reconsider his decision. I told him that if we did not get the loan, that we would lose everything. We would lose the church! I quoted every Scripture I could think of, but still he wouldn't change his mind. *What is going to happen now?* I thought. Those were times when my faith was being tested to the limit.

I called my brother-in-law, Mickey Caldwell, and my father-in-law, Tommy Grant, and told them what had happened. I asked them to pray with me, that we could find someone with as large of financial statement as the one we were losing. They knew that if we did not, that we would be losing the church.

About eight thirty that evening, Mickey called and asked if I remembered a man in Okeene, Oklahoma, for whom we had worked several years before. Tommy, my father-in-law, had built a nursing home for the man, and Mickey and I had been working for Tommy at the time. After we had finished the nursing home, Mickey and I had stayed and remodeled a building for his wife's new dress store.

Mickey told me he had called the man and told him what we needed. The man asked if Tommy, Mickey, and I had signed the note and pledged our financial statements. Mickey told him that we had. He said that was good enough for him, and if we would bring the papers Monday morning, he would give us his financial statement and sign the note for us. We were there before eight on Monday morning.

When we sat down, he gave me his financial statement

and asked if it would be large enough for what we needed. I looked at the net worth and it was almost three times as large as the one we had lost! He then signed the papers we had brought, and we took them back to Oklahoma City. The Lord had performed another miracle! The man was a member of the Baptist church. He has never stepped inside Faith Tabernacle! Yet the Lord used him to keep us from losing our church! Another mountain had been removed. Our faith was growing!

Seven months had passed before we secured the money to complete the church. The first thing we had to do was pay off all of the bonds so that we could have a first mortgage on the church. As a result of the long delay, the contractors were unable to keep their contracts with the church. More than a year had passed since we started and the cost had escaladed considerably. It soon became apparent that the loan we had secured would not be enough to finish the job.

We discussed what we were going to do to finish the church. It was decided to self-finance. I went to the Oklahoma Securities Commission and found out what was necessary for us to do that. We sold notes to people in the church at a higher rate of interest than they could get at the banks or savings and loans. The notes were to be secured by the integrity of the church. That was necessary since there was already a first mortgage on the property. The response of the church people was amazing. We were finally able to finish the new facility.

We had sold the old church during this time, giving us additional money. When everything was completed, we had 72,000 square feet of buildings, which included a sanctuary seating 2000 and educational facilities for that many people. The total cost was $2,750,000. That was a cost of $38.19 a square foot. The price included the property, the pews, the sound system, and all the parking, a complete turn-key job.

At last, on Sunday, September 3, 1978, we had our first service in the new sanctuary! There were 825 in attendance. My first message was, "Whosoever Will May Come." Sixteen gave their hearts to the Lord. I baptized fifteen in water, and took in twenty-eight new members. It was truly a glorious day in Faith Tabernacle's history. We were having an exciting journey of faith.

The first wedding in our new sanctuary was Friday, the 13th of October, of that year. Otis Garrison and Charletta Phillips was the first couple I married.

We set October 15th as the date for the dedication of our new church. I had contacted Thomas F. Zimmerman, the General Superintendent of the Assemblies of God, to be our dedicatory speaker. However, Brother Zimmerman had to have open-heart surgery and was unable to come. Don Brankel had been a great blessing to us in many revivals, so I contacted him to dedicate the church.

Sunday, October 15, 1978 was a great day at Faith Tabernacle. The day of dedication had finally arrived. More than 1000 were in attendance. The call to worship began with Bill Hedrick, our Minister of Music, directing the choir and orchestra in "Bless the Lord." Melvin Decker, one of our board members, read the Scripture. Dr. S. J. Scott, the former pastor, gave the Invocation. I was so thrilled that Brother and Sister Scott were able to be with us on that glorious occasion. They had done so much for the church and brought it through a very difficult time. Scott Taylor led the congregation in "All Hail the Power." Linwood Carr, our Minister of Youth, made acknowledgements of the many people who had helped in the building of the church. The Faith Company, a talented and anointed group, did special music from the church. Then Gretnia and I sang the song I had written, "Faith Can Move Mountains." If there was ever a song that was appropriate, it was that song. The Lord had indeed moved many mountains for us in our building project. Rev. Don Brankel brought the dedicatorial message. I led the congregation in the Act of Dedication. Don Brankel prayed the Prayer of Dedication. Scott Taylor led the congregation in "To God Be the Glory." Then Dr. Robert E. Goggin, the District Superintendent of the Oklahoma District Council of the Assemblies of God, prayed the prayer of Benediction. What a great day!!

Vicki Jamison came and conducted a five-night revival in November and Mike Warnke came for two great services. Gretnia wrote and produced a beautiful Christmas drama entitled, "King of Love." Gretnia had been deeply involved every year we were at Faith Tabernacle, writing and producing our Christmas pageants. She had learned well the things that Sister Scott had taught her. We always had great crowds, and had wonderful results when I gave the invitations at the end of the programs. That was the first year in our new sanctuary and it was wonderful having the additional room on the platform, as well as the three different stage areas for the dramas. Gretnia and Rev. Russell Pratt painted some beautiful backdrops for the productions.

Don Brankel was scheduled to start revival the first week of January in 1979. However, there was a big snowstorm and we put the meeting off until March.

The second wedding I conducted was for Kenny, our son, and Kathy Tolson. Their wedding was February 2nd, 1979. I was proud that they had a beautiful sanctuary in which to have their wedding.

Brother and Sister Scott came and preached for us in March. I was so thrilled that they could be with us and enjoy the blessings of their faithful ministry at the church. I was always honored to have them come and minister to the church. They were always a great blessing to us.

We experienced some tight times in getting the money to take care of the added cost in operating such a big, new church. There were times when I had to raise additional money to take care of special things. On one such occasion the Lord spoke to my heart to give what Gretnia and I had in our savings. It was not all that much, but for us, it was a lot. We had sold a house and had put the money in savings. We had both of our children in college, which was expensive and the church had not been able to give us a raise for quite some time. Despite these things, I had learned many years before that if the Lord asks you to do something He will take care of you. I watched in amazement, as the Lord supplied the needs for Kenny and Tammy's school bills. I learned through obedience, that He will supply all my needs. He allowed my faith to be tested again.

Sunday, September 16th was a great day for us at the church. I had told everyone that we would not open the balcony until the bottom floor was completely full. Mike Warnke was our special guest that day. Sunday morning we had 1054 in attendance. I watched as people began coming in on Sunday evening. I waited until the bottom floor was completely full, and then I told the ushers to open the balcony. Gretnia and I stood there and watched the balcony fill to capacity. There were more than 1400 on the bottom floor and the balcony held more than 600. We then opened the choir for seating and then had to put up folding chairs in order to seat everyone. I cannot tell you the feeling Gretnia and I had when we saw the church packed to capacity! There were more than 2100 in attendance that night and when Mike Warnke gave the invitation, more than 100 came forward to give their hearts to the Lord! It was wonderful seeing the church filled and seeing so many coming to the altar.

1979 was a blessed year. We had over 2500 visitors. 339 gave their hearts to the Lord in our altars. We had miracles of healings. The Lord had truly honored our faith and commitment to Him in building the church.

In the fall of that same year, Tammy, our daughter, started attending Evangel University in Springfield. On Friday, January 11, 1980 while helping Tammy load her car so she could return to start her new semester, I thought I was having a bad case of indigestion. It turned out to be more than that. Over the next couple of days I began experiencing dizziness and light-headiness.

I preached both services, Sunday the 13th. There were times when I had to hold on to the pulpit because I was so light-headed. I thought perhaps that I had hypoglycemia. I asked

Juanita Stewart, one of the ladies in the church who worked for a doctor, if she could get in touch with the doctor and schedule me for tests the next day. She was able to do so. The next day I drove to Mercy Hospital to begin the tests. The first thing they did was take my blood pressure. In just a few minutes they came in to do an EKG on me—that was not on the schedule they had given me.

In a few more minutes the doctor came in and began asking me questions. He wanted to know what I had been doing. I told him about completing the massive building program at the church. He then informed me that when they had taken my blood pressure, it was so high that they were afraid I was going to have a stroke. When they had done the EKG, it revealed that I had had a heart attack sometime within the previous three to five days. The indigestion I thought I had was really a heart attack! He then told me that he was putting me in Intensive Care. I felt like someone who had just been arrested. I asked him if I could make one phone call. I started to get off the table and go to the phone. He informed me I could not get up. He said, "I will dial the number for you." I gave him my home phone number. When Gretnia answered, I told her I would not be coming home, because they were admitting me and I would be in ICU.

On Wednesday morning, January 16th, the nurse came in at 6:00 A.M. to do an enzyme test to see if my heart was still showing evidence of damage being done. A few minutes after she left, I must have passed out, because the next thing I remember the doctors and nurses had rushed into my room. As they all converged on my room, they began working frantically on me to keep me alive. I could hear everything that was going on, but I could not talk.

They worked on me all that day until about 2:00 P.M. As I lay there, I can tell you I was searching my heart to see if there was anything for which I needed forgiveness. When you realize that the next breath you breathe may be your last, you don't want anything between you and the Savior. The Lord gave me the words of a song with that very thought, while I was lying there.

"NOTHING BETWEEN MY SOUL AND MY SAVIOR"
KENNETH MCGEE

Verse one:
> The time is drawing near,
> when our Lord shall soon appear.
> He will split those Eastern skies.
> We will see Him through tear-dimmed eyes.

Verse two:
> Oh, our King is coming at last.
> I've just heard the trumpet's blast.
> He's coming just as He said,
> to take the living with the dead.

Chorus:
> Oh, there's nothing between my soul and my Savior,
> There's nothing between, to keep me from His favor.
> Every sin has been covered by the blood of the Lamb.
> Now there's nothing between my soul and my Savior.

Verse three:
> Oh, can't you feel within your breast,
> that you have passed the test.
> And, what our Lord said He would do,
> Yes, is finally coming true.

Gretnia and Kenny came in during the visitor's hours at two o'clock that afternoon, and while they were there, I began having severe problems again. I heard the staff tell Gretnia and Kenny that they would have to leave, because they were losing me. I heard Gretnia, as she began crying, say to Kenny, "We must leave because Daddy is not going to make it!"

Within a few minutes of them leaving, I had another visitor! He did not stop at the nurse's station to see if it was all right for Him to come in. He simply walked into my room and put His hand over my heart. As He touched me, I felt a warmth go throughout my body. I had not seen Him; I had just felt His touch! Immediately, I was awake! My blood pressure became normal! I rose up in bed and told them I was hungry! After all, I had not had anything to eat all day long!

Needless to say, the doctors and nurses were amazed at what had just happened. The Chief of Staff of Mercy Hospital was my heart doctor. He told me that he would like to do an arterialgram on me to see what had happened. I told him that would be fine, but I wanted him to know that the Lord had touched me.

The next day they took me down to the heart cauterization unit where they did the arterialgram. The doctor told me when he started that he would be 90% sure of what my problem was as the test was being done. When he finished the test, he had this strange look on his face. He said, "Kenneth, I don't see anything wrong with you, but I want the radiologist to look this over before I tell you for sure."

Two hours later, he and my regular MD came into my room with their report. He told me that they knew what had brought me into the hospital, and what had happened to me since I had been in the hospital, but that the arterialgram had revealed that nothing was wrong with my heart! He told me that there was no evidence of blockage, no evidence of heart damage and no evidence of heart disease! Then he meddled a little bit, because he told me if I would lose about twenty pounds, and go on a regular exercise program, that I should live to a ripe old age!

That was twenty-five years ago this past January 16th, 2005. I have played basketball, gone big-game hunting, and done just about anything I have wanted to do! Praise the Lord for His healing touch! My faith was growing by leaps and bounds!

I will never forget the first Sunday I was able to preach after my heart attack. The doctor would not let me preach for six weeks, even though the Lord had healed me. So, when I went to the pulpit to preach, I guess everyone expected me to be quiet and reserved. That was not the case. I was so pumped up at getting to preach, that I jumped up and down during my message. You could hear the gasps from the congregation—I know they were expecting me to have another heart attack.

Dan Betzer came in March to preach a revival. Brother Betzer was the radio speaker for *Revivaltime,* the national radio broadcast of the Assemblies of God. His ministry was a tremendous blessing to the church. I still have people tell me about some of his sermons that touched their lives.

John G. Hall came to us in June for a revival. Brother Hall, in my opinion, is the greatest Bible prophecy preacher in the Assemblies of God. I do not know how many times I have had him for revivals all down through the years.

Jerry B. Walker came back to Faith for a revival in November. One hundred and fifty were saved and thirty were filled with the Holy Ghost in his meeting.

Gretnia presented another beautiful Christmas Pageant entitled, "The King is Coming." It was presented two times with wonderful results in the altars, as people gave their hearts to the Lord. 1980 had been another amazing year in our new facility.

1981 proved to be yet another exciting year for us. Gretnia and I were asked to host the "Oklahoma Alive" praise program for TBN on channel 14. That was a very rewarding experience that we will never forget. Duane and Lisa Brogdon became our youth pastors that year. Under their leadership, the youth grew by leaps and bounds. We had a steady stream of anointed speakers during the year.

Gretnia and I celebrated our twenty-fifth wedding anniversary on December 29th. We had seen more than 400 saved and 100 filled with the Holy Spirit during the year. And, once again, we had more than 2500 visitors to the church.

1982 started out in high gear. Duane and Lisa were having tremendous crowds in the youth and many were being saved in each of their services. Don Brankel was with us for our annual revival with him. We always had a wonderful outpouring of the Holy Spirit in his revivals. I was invited to preach a seminar on the Holy Spirit for Calvary Temple, which was located in Denver, Colorado. The services were held in Colorado Springs in a beautiful facility called, Glen Erie Castle. Everyone who attended the seminar received the baptism of the Holy Spirit! There was even one couple who had come to the seminar who professed to be atheists. They too were saved and filled with the Holy Spirit!

On April 4th, Gretnia and I celebrated our 13th anniversary at the church. On April 7th, Lisa Whelchel, TV personality, spoke in the youth service. There were so many in attendance that they had to come into the sanctuary. There were more than 850 in that youth service! We had 928 in attendance that following Sunday, which was Easter. We had not done anything special that day. People just came to worship the Lord!

Gretnia and I were continuing to host the "Praise" program for TBN. In September, one of our guests was a man who had not been raised in Pentecost. However, he had been filled with the Holy Spirit, and was testifying about his newfound experience. At the end of the telecast, he came and told me that the Lord had spoken something to him, and that he would like to make an appointment with me and tell me what the Lord had said to him about me. I set a time for us to meet, and he told me he would be at the church at that time.

The day we were to meet, I received a call from John G. Hall, who wanted to take me to lunch. I told him I could meet him, but that I had to be back to the church in time to meet the other man with whom I had made the previous engagement. Brother Hall told me at lunch that I should not be afraid to trust the Lord, if He were to ask me to go back on the evangelistic field. He told me that he and Sister Hall had been praying and that the Lord wanted them to share that with me. I thought, *How strange,* because I had not shared with anyone what I had been feeling about leaving the church and going back on the field.

I went back to the church to meet with the other gentleman. When he came into my office, he told me that what he was going to share with me would only be true, if the Lord had already been dealing with my heart about it. Well, that is exactly the way I believe it. The Lord will always work on both ends of the line. He told me that during the TV program the Lord had spoken to his heart about me. He said that the Lord had shown him that I would be "going out and coming in." That is exactly what an evangelist does. He goes out and comes in. He told me not to be afraid to trust the Lord if that is what I began doing. I thought, *Wow, in the mouth of two or three witnesses' let every word be established*. I thanked him for coming and being obedient to what the Lord had asked him to do. And then, he left.

I then went to my secretary and told her I was going into the sanctuary to pray and that I did not want to be disturbed. I had to hear from the Lord! I began pouring my heart out to the Lord, and told Him that I did not want to miss His perfect will for my life. I thanked Him for the privilege I had of being the pastor of such a wonderful church. But, I told Him that I would only do what He wanted me to do. I was crying and felt as though my heart was going to come out of my chest. I don't remember how long I prayed, but I completely surrendered my will into His will. I told Him that I would like to have one more confirmation about His will, if He didn't mind. I asked the Lord to have Rev. Armon Newburn, a close friend of mine, who at that time had never asked me for a revival, to be the first one to ask me for a revival meeting. I finished my prayer time and went back to my office to think about everything that had happened that day.

Just a couple of days later, I received a call from Brother Newburn's secretary, asking me to come to Tulsa the following Tuesday, for a committee meeting, of which both of us were a member. I thought, *How strange this is, that he would call and want us to meet*. The following Tuesday, I began driving across the Turner Turnpike, making my way to meet Brother

Newburn. I cried and prayed all the way across the turnpike. I had the strangest sensation in my heart.

Our committee met and as we were breaking up, Brother Newburn asked if I would stay and visit with him for a little while. We went into his office and began talking. He looked at me and asked if I could come and preach a revival for him. Well, a person can ask that question, and never set a date, and you may never preach him a revival. So, I laughed and asked him if he had a date in mind. He took his date book out and set a time for me to come for a revival. I broke, and told him how I had prayed, and that I would be resigning the next Sunday, because the Lord had given me my other confirmation.

I cried and prayed all the way back across the turnpike, because I knew that it would not be easy to resign Faith Tabernacle. I knew that it would be hard for some of my family to understand what the Lord was doing in our lives. The Lord had always led me up until that point in my life, and I knew that He was leading me still. It is in times like these when your faith is tested. Your faith is tested to see if you can hear that still, small voice amid the clamor of all of the other voices. There wasn't a doubt in my mind about what the Lord wanted, because He had sent two men to tell me what was going to happen, and then He had answered my cry for another confirmation. The following Sunday morning, September 26, 1982, I resigned effective November 7, 1982.

We had been at the church for more than 14 years. We had seen Him perform miracle after miracle in getting the new church built. We had seen the church completely full. We had never missed a payment, nor were we ever a day late on a payment. Those 14 years were the most memorable in our lives. Our kids grew up while we were there. We will never forget the most wonderful days of our lives.

We had been tremendously blessed with great associates. **Steve and Vada Allen,** who were our first associates, are now pastors of Oak Hill Assembly of God in Nashville, Tennessee.

Dean and Peggy Galyen are now missionaries in Zimbabwe, Africa. **Jim and Linda McNabb** are now pastors of the great "The Bridge," formally, Mustang Assembly of God in Mustang, Oklahoma. Jim also serves as the Assistant Superintendent of the Oklahoma District. **Bruce and Pam Chambers** are pastors of Faith Tabernacle in Aurora, Colorado. **Bill and Vera Hedrick**, who had been our Ministers of Music, are retired, living in Oklahoma City. **Duane and Lisa Brogdon** are pastors of Tulsa Hope Worship Center, Tulsa, Oklahoma. **Linwood and Marilyn Carr** were our youth pastors for several years. Linwood has passed away, but Marilyn still lives in Oklahoma City. **Bill Shell,** who had been my Business Administrator and Christian Educational Director, and his wife **Retha** are retired and live in Oklahoma City. I don't know if I could have made it without his encouraging words of wisdom and advice. He was a tremendous blessing to me.

Tom Greene, who is now the National Director of Men's Ministries and Light for the Lost, lives in Springfield, Missouri, with his wife **Pam**. Tom was called to preach, January 21, 1973 at Faith Tabernacle. When he went home that night, he told his folks what had happened in the service. His mother, Loretta, told him to go on to bed; that he would feel better the next day. His dad, Bobby, told him the next morning that he had better go ahead and finish his schooling, so he would have something to fall back on, just in case the ministry didn't work out for him. Tom and Pam served as our youth pastors for two years. We can all testify to what the Lord has done in Tom and Pam's lives. I am extremely proud of them!

It was always my policy, as pastor, to take the young people, who had been called into the ministry, and help them get started in the ministry. I would take them around to meet other pastors, and introduce them. I would give them an opportunity to preach. I would encourage them to start getting the information needed to start in the ministry.

Gloria Fajardo is now pastor of Cathedral of the Palms,

in Corpus Christi, Texas. She and her husband, **David** came out of Faith Tabernacle. I had Gloria lead the women's prayer meetings for the church. She became an outstanding evangelist, greatly used by the Holy Spirit.

I have had the privilege of preaching revivals for all of my former associates. To me, that is a great honor.

November 7, 1982 was a day I will never forget. The church had received a special offering to purchase a new van for our evangelistic ministry. More than $20,000 was given in the offering. They gave us a beautiful, burgundy and gray, customized Dodge van with gray leather interior. The van had four captain's chairs and a bench seat that made out into a bed. It was a tremendous blessing to Gretnia and me in our ministry. It was not easy, leaving a place where we had a good income and were being well taken care of. We were going back on the evangelistic field, where you literally live by faith, week by week. The Lord had always proven Himself in supplying all of our needs though, and I knew He would be with us in our new venture of faith.

I could never thank the Lord enough for allowing Gretnia and me the privilege of being pastors of our home church. To God Be the Glory! What a wonderful adventure of faith it was!

Romans 10:17 states, **"So then faith cometh by hearing, and hearing by the word of God."** I know that faith comes by the Word of God, but it also comes through the Lord performing miracles and answering our prayers. He had done that from the time we went to Faith Tabernacle, until we left. Faith had moved many mountains!

It was a wonderful privilege to have our family in the church. They lived the many wonderful experiences with Gretnia and me. I have asked Kenny, our son, and Tammy, our daughter to share their memories of our times in the ministry.

KENNY'S MEMORIES

When my dad asked me to write a few words about my thoughts concerning his new book on faith, and the history of his life living in faith, I really struggled with what to say and share. During a recent devotion and prayer time, however, the thought came to me that while being blessed to have been raised in a Christian home, where we lived by faith each and every day, I had to come to the realization and belief that a life of faith was real and that it was what I wanted in my life and for my own family.

As I reflected on my life, there were three significant events that impacted my life and solidified my faith in God. Remarkably, the events seemed to come during times in my life that historically are defining ages for each of us.

The first event happened when I was thirteen or fourteen years of age. This is a time when, as a teenager, we start to really question the faith that has been taught to us and a time when we also try to gain our own independence regarding what we believe. I had been saved at a young age and was serving the Lord when I witnessed a miracle that just made my faith in the Lord that much more real. It was a Sunday morning. My dad prayed for an elderly gentleman who had been blind for more than thirty years and the Lord healed him right in front of my eyes. He could see and at that moment there was no doubt that I believed that the Lord could do anything—that nothing was impossible with God!

The second event happened when I was twenty-two. Again, at another time in our lives when we try to determine, once we are on our own and away from our parents influence, whether we really believe in a miracle-working God. I had gotten married and my wife and I were expecting our first child when I received a call that my dad had experienced a heart attack. We all rushed to the hospital to find he was in intensive care. My mom and I went in to see my dad during the fifteen-minute-per-hour visitation time and I couldn't believe what I saw. My dad was not conscious, and he was so still that his self-winding watch had stopped. The doctors had told us that he had experienced a massive heart attack and we did not know if he would survive.

My mom and I went back to the waiting room where there were a number of people waiting with us and we started to pray. We waited for what seemed like forever until the next visitation time allowed us to go and see my father again. This time, when my mom and I went into the room, again I could not believe my eyes. I was thrilled to see my dad alert and awake as if everything was fine. The next day, my dad was taken in for an arteriogram to check out the damage done to his heart and no damage was found. God had done a miracle, and again there was no doubt that I believed that the Lord could do anything—that nothing was impossible with God!

The third event happened when I was thirty-three years old. This event was the turning point in my life and was a trial of the faith that I had developed in my earlier years. In most cases, men in their late twenties through their early thirties are establishing their careers, building toward success, and developing their families. It is a time of life in which you can easily get busy, gain confidence in your own abilities, and can put the Lord on the back burner. In my life, the Lord had blessed me with a wonderful wife, three beautiful daughters, and a profitable position in my career. Fortunately, the development of my faith had kept me close to the Lord, but I also felt that I was talented in my ability to make money.

Over a two and one-half year period, I became ill to the point that it put me in the hospital on three different occasions.

In addition, the company I was working for started experiencing financial difficulties, and I was forced to look for different employment. During this time, God was faithful, but He also allowed me to determine if my faith was real or not. It was a time to trust in Him and not in my own abilities.

After recovering from my illness, I accepted a great position with another company. It was a dream position within my field. Although, I testified to the Lord's faithfulness, I could not help but believe that my talents were a major factor in my success of obtaining this position. The Lord had a different plan in mind, however, because within six months I resigned from this dream position and had to start looking for different employment.

Over the next year, no matter what I tried, nothing seemed to open up. Real estate values in Oklahoma City deflated. My wife and I lost our home, our cars, and everything we had that had reflected our earlier success. My wife and I had a choice to make during this time. We could blame God for causing us to lose everything, or we could continue in our faith and trust that He would see us through. My wife and I chose to trust God. You see, I had seen a blind man miraculously healed; I had seen my dad miraculously healed. I knew that God was faithful. My heritage supported this faith.

As my wife and I prayed, we both expressed separately to the Lord that He could take everything we owned as long as He didn't take our girls. One Sunday night after church, I had gone to bed and was awakened during the night by a loud scream from my wife. I knew something had to be wrong with my middle daughter, Kamber, because I had been so burdened for her during my prayer time over the previous week. I rushed to the kitchen and I saw my wife and daughter standing there. My wife told me that Kamber could not breathe, that she was having an asthma attack, and that she could not locate her inhaler. I immediately prayed for Kamber through the power of the precious blood of Jesus and Kamber was instantly healed. She started breathing normally, laid on the couch, and went to sleep.

As my wife and I started reflecting on what had just happened, my wife told me that God had woken her up during the night telling her to go find Kamber. Kamber did not have the air to speak or the strength to find us. My wife found her searching for her inhaler when she screamed out for me. As we talked about the miracle, I knew within my heart that the period of trial we had been experiencing over the last two and one-half years was going to end. Within a few short weeks, I picked up a profitable consulting account. Work started pouring in and God began restoring everything we lost, plus more than we could imagine.

When my wife and I looked back at the years during this time, we realized that although we had lost everything financially, God was faithful in supplying our needs. Our daughters' feet did not grow for more than a year and we did not have to buy shoes. Our limited funds, after paying our tithes, were always just enough.

Surviving this event was a result of the faith that I had developed growing up in a Christian home, seeing miracles within my family, and enduring trials that define our trust in God. Through all of these events, I believed that the Lord could do anything. I believed that with God nothing is impossible. I still believe it today! Now it is time for my faith heritage to be passed on to my daughters.

TAMMY'S MEMORIES

I was too young to remember much about the church dad pastored in El Reno, Oklahoma. Most of my memories were of the years at Faith Tabernacle (Faith). Faith was a wonderful church that had a lot of great people. I would like to share with you some of my fondest memories.

The first person that comes to mind is Sis. Burton. She was my Sunday School teacher when I was little. What I remember most was going to her house and spending Sunday afternoon with her. She would take me home after the morning service and bring me back for the evening service. I would help her fix lunch. She taught me how to make meatloaf. Then we would play a little and take a nap. What a sweet woman! I will never forget her.

My next memory is of Chief McPherson. I loved Chief McPherson! He scared me at first with his Indian costume, but then I came to love him so much that I did not get scared anymore. I used to love watching him draw pictures. I would sit mesmerized while he told a story and drew a picture. He gave out Indian money called, wampum, to those who brought other children to Vacation Bible School. I remember always wanting to win his wampum so that I could go shopping in his store. Boy, those were the days! I always looked forward to VBS, especially if Chief McPherson was going to be there.

My next memory is of Jerry B. Walker's revival. I remember seeing miracles with my own eyes that to this day I still cannot believe happened. When I tell people that I saw miracles growing up, they do not believe me. But I did! I saw

people walk who were on crutches and in wheelchairs. I saw
deaf people healed. They could hear! I saw large tumors disappear right before my eyes. It was miraculous! And, to see the
church so full and overflowing was a magnificent sight as well.

And speaking of miracles, the one miracle that has stayed
with me the most happened in a regular Sunday morning service.
Dad asked for people to come forward who needed healing. A
man came forward who was blind. I can remember this so viv-
idly. The man asked for healing of his sight. Dad prayed for him
and I remember dad asking him if he could see light. The man
grabbed dad by the shoulders and said, "Light? Preacher, I can
see you!" WOW! That whole church came unglued! I still get
goose bumps just thinking about it.

I also remember the revivals with Don Brankel. I loved
Bro. Brankel—still do! He is the most positive person I know. I
just love being around him. You cannot be down when you are
with Bro. Brankel. He is so uplifting to be around. And he makes
me laugh. I remember the first time I heard him sing, "I'm so
glad He let me in . . ." I was afraid to laugh because he couldn't
sing very well, but then he started laughing as he was singing. I
loved that! He was a genuine Christian! He was real!

I remember John G. Hall and his prophecy chart. I used
to look forward to his services because I would learn so much.
His chart was a magnificent sight stretching across the stage. I
would sit in awe as he spoke because Bro. Hall knew the Bible.
I was always impressed at how he could quote the scriptures and
answer any question given to him.

The next person I have great memories of was a man
who (at the time) I could not believe my dad actually brought
to the church. We had been listening to his records and tapes,
so I was really looking forward to seeing him in person. He was
so funny. And he had a great testimony. But, the first time he
walked out on stage I about died! He had long hair, big glasses,
and shabby clothes. I know my dad must have cringed when
he saw him at the airport. The man I am referring to is Mike

Warnke. Mike Warnke turned out to be one of my favorite people. He helped shatter the image of what Christians should look and talk like. He was so down-to-earth. He just told it like it was. What an amazing man and ministry! He could reach people you or I could never reach. I wanted to be like him. I wanted to be able to reach people in "my world." He taught me how to do that. I will always be thankful to Mike Warnke for showing me true Christianity.

We also had wonderful concerts at Faith. I loved music and the groups that came to perform because they left a lasting impression on me. Groups like The Downings, Andrae Crouch & The Disciples, and The Imperials, to name a few. They would pack the church out and we had great services when they were there.

The other part of Faith that gives me wonderful memories was the way we socialized with each other. We would go out to lunch after Sunday morning services, go out to dinner after Sunday evening services, and go out to dinner before church on Wednesday night. There was always a big group of us. And when sports activities were going on, whether it was in the gym or on a softball field, there was always a large group of people at every game. We had a blast!

I have great memories of our ski trips too. Crested Butte, Colorado—a little taste of Heaven! We had so much fun on our ski trips. We took busloads and stayed right on the slopes. We would snow ski all day and then play games at night. The card game, Rook, was the game of choice at that time. We played Rook everywhere—on the bus and in the rooms. What wonderful memories!

I could go on and on with my memories. There were many people too numerous to mention who crossed my path at Faith and made a difference in my life . . . people who changed my life. I would not be here today if it were not for those people who prayed me through my struggles in life. I know there were bad times too, but the good times far outweigh the bad times.

My years at Faith Tabernacle were a time in my life that I will always treasure! The people and memories I will never forget!

Chapter Eight
ON THE ROAD AGAIN

Another new chapter was beginning for us. Gretnia and I left on November 8th (the Monday after our last Sunday at Faith) for another trip to the Holy Land. I felt it was good timing to be out of the country after such a traumatic day in leaving the church. The time away proved to be a great blessing to us.

After we returned from the Holy Land, we had revivals in Verdigris, Oklahoma, and in St. Louis, Missouri. The pastor of Verdigris had accompanied us on the trip to the Holy Land, and had invited us to come for the revival when we returned. And Dean Galyen, who had been our youth pastor for four years at Faith Tabernacle, had invited us to come to end the year at his church in Missouri. It was evident that our lives were going to be different than they had been for the fourteen years we had been at Faith Tabernacle, but the journey of faith is always exciting and we were ready to embark on it.

I recorded a new singing tape in December. I put ten songs that were special to me on the tape. I entitled the new tape, **"Ken McGee Sings Praises to the King."** The songs were: "He Was There All The Time," "It Is Finished," "I Call Him Lord," "Behold The Lamb," "Blessed Assurance," "Leavin' On My Mind," "Surely The Presence," "When He Reached Down His Hand For Me," "Adoration," and "Gone." It is still one of my best sellers today.

We entered into 1983 with great enthusiasm. The Lord was opening doors for revivals and we were traveling all over the country. It was exciting to see people giving their hearts to the Lord. Many were being filled with the Holy Spirit. We were experiencing a number of miraculous healings. We decided to record a new singing tape. We recorded ten songs and entitled the tape, **"From Our House to Yours."** Kenny and Tammy, our son and daughter, each recorded two songs on the tape. Kenny recorded "He's Alive" and "Because Of Whose I Am." Tammy recorded, "He Is the King" and "Didn't He Shine?" I was thrilled to have them help me on the project. They both have tremendous voices. I was and still am extremely proud of both of them. I recorded the songs: "Sacrifice Of Praise," "He Touched Me," "Eastern Gate," "Whatever It Takes," "Love Lifted Me," and "My House Is Full."

That summer Gretnia and I took our family on vacation to Callaway Gardens, which is between Columbus and Atlanta, in Georgia, and then, on to Disney World in Orlando, Florida. We had always wanted our kids to feel that the ministry was a blessing. We never wanted them to look back at our lives and feel as though they had missed out on a lot of things. We always enjoyed our vacations. Gretnia's mom and dad, as well as Gretnia's sister, Carol, and her family were with us on this particular one.

After the vacation, it was time to get ready for General Council in Anaheim, California. Don and Neta Brankel, our close friends who had preached a number of revivals for us, met Gretnia and me in Oklahoma City. We drove together in our custom van. Don and I rode in the front seat and preached to each other most of the way to California. Gretnia and Neta sat in the back and talked about sewing and grandkids. It seemed like the van began pulling to the side every time we passed an ice cream store. It was hard to pass any place that sold ice cream.

I had been asked to serve on the Teller's Committee for the General Council that year. The subject of "Divorce and Remarriage" was debated and voted on in that council. I don't know when I have ever heard such heartbreaking stories, as I heard on that occasion. The resolution did not pass, even though there was heated debate. After the General Council concluded, Don, Neta, Gretnia and I went to Northern California to preach. I had services scheduled with Gretnia's uncle, and Don had services scheduled with a friend of his. We were to spend the next night with friends of Don and Neta.

Don's friend had an earth-moving company. When we arrived at their house, he told Don that he had a big contract with the state of California, and that he was having trouble with his equipment breaking down. He told us that due to a clause in his contract, if his trouble continued he would lose a great sum of money. He took us to his job site, where there were a number of huge, earth-moving machines all lined up, ready to begin work the next day. He then asked Don and me if we would anoint the machinery and pray that they would not break down anymore. We took anointing oil and began anointing and praying for each piece of machinery, asking the Lord to keep them operating until the job was completed. After that, not one piece of machinery broke down until the job was completed! The Lord is faithful! He knows the things we have need of, even before we ask **(Matthew 6:8)**. God's Word states that we have not, simply because we ask not **(James 4:2)**. Sometimes we may think that the Lord is not interested in the things we pray for. Seeing that the Lord had prevented those machines from breaking down was a great experience for me. It boosted my faith level. It helped me to discover that the Lord is consistent in all of His promises, no matter how foolish they may appear to others.

Don's friend took us to Carmel, California. He had done the dirt work for a famous, beautiful golf course there. As a result, Don and I were able to play the course without any cost to us. That was a wonderful blessing, because the green fees were very high. The breeze from the ocean became quite cool while we were playing and so we each bought a chartreuse green pullover sweater to wear in order to stay warm. Everyone could see us coming!

By the time the four of us had gotten back to Oklahoma City, we had been together for two full weeks. It is easy for people to get on each other's nerves, but we had had the most wonderful time being together. We had never grown tired of each other. Don and Neta Brankel are truly some of our best friends.

I began 1984 with a revival in Sapulpa, Oklahoma. During the revival I began having a dream about starting a new church in the Oklahoma City area. It was something from which I could not get away. The Lord had even given me the name of the church—Trinity Church. When I got back to Oklahoma City, I looked in the phone book to see if there was a Trinity Assembly of God church in the area. There was not.

I thought that this entire happening was really strange. After all, I had spent fourteen wonderful years at Faith Tabernacle, and I had not thought about starting another church in the area. I must admit however, that I had always wanted to start a church from scratch. I had heard so many stories of men doing something like that for the Lord. In fact, back when Gretnia and I had gone to the church in El Reno, Rev. Robert E. Goggin, our District Superintendent, had offered to let me use the district auditorium, if I would start a new church in the area. I had not felt that it was the will of the Lord for our lives at that time, however.

I knew that all of this would require a great deal of prayer. My next revival was in San Angelo, Texas. While in the revival I spent a great deal of time in prayer. I knew that I must have a fresh anointing for the revival and, I knew that I must hear from the Lord about the new church in Oklahoma City. When I got back to Oklahoma City, I told Gretnia how the Lord had been dealing with my heart. Instead of acting on my inclinations at that time, however, I put off my decision until a later time.

It was shortly after that time that I decided to record another singing tape. Our revivals were going well and the Lord was blessing in our services. I always liked to have fresh songs available in our services and so we recorded the new tape, **"We**

Love To Tell the Story." I again asked Kenny, our son, and Tammy, our daughter, to help me on the tape. Kenny recorded: "The Highest Praise," and "They Could Not." Tammy recorded: "Farther and Higher," and "I Go to the Rock." Then the two of them recorded, "Jesus Never Fails." I recorded: "Our God Reigns," "I Love to Tell the Story," "Will the Circle Be Unbroken?" "Only the Redeemed," and "Light At the End of the Darkness."

In April of 1984 I began having severe pain when I would go to the bathroom. I thought I had hemorrhoids, but that proved not to be the case. That same month, as I was driving to Universal City, Texas for my next revival, I put the new demo tape of our recording in the car's cassette player. I was in pain the entire trip, even though I was sitting on a pillow. I had just passed the intersection, south of Waco, where you turn to go to the air base, when Kenny and Tammy's song, "Jesus Never Fails," came on. As I listened to the words of their song, all heaven came down in the car. I began praising the Lord and speaking in tongues as the Holy Spirit flooded my soul. I don't remember too much about the rest of the trip, because I was simply lost in the Spirit. The Lord did not heal me at that time, even though the pain was gone while they were singing. He had just blessed me!

Following my trip to Texas I was to fly to California for my next four revivals. After the four revivals in California, I was to fly back to Oklahoma for my fifth revival which was to be held in Mannford. Before I left, I went to my doctor to see what was causing my pain. He told me that if my condition did not improve while I was gone, that he would have to do surgery when I returned.

My first meeting was in Colton, California. When I flew in on Saturday, the pastor and his wife picked me up from the airport and took me to eat at a Mexican restaurant. When we were on our way to the restaurant he told me that he was ending a forty day fast. I could hardly believe my ears! He had not eaten for forty days and he was going to eat Mexican food?! (By the way, he did not suffer indigestion, or any other problems.)

I told him that I was excited to be the evangelist for his meeting if he had fasted for forty days, and he told me that some of his deacons had also fasted for twenty one days. Upon hearing that, I knew that there was no telling what the Lord was going to do in the revival. In fact, I don't know if it really mattered who the evangelist was, because I knew that the Lord had great things in store for that meeting.

The services on Sunday were exciting. People were saved and filled with the Holy Spirit as I preached about being filled with the baptism of the Holy Spirit. Monday night I preached on the subject, "The Benefit of Speaking in Other Tongues." When I gave the invitation, a young lady about eleven years old came forward for prayer. I asked her what she wanted the Lord to do for her. She told me that she wanted to receive the baptism of the Holy Spirit. I had noticed when she came forward for prayer that she walked with a noticeable limp. When I asked her to raise her hands to praise the Lord, I noticed that she was only able to raise one of her arms fully; she could only raise the other arm part way. I found out later that she had born breech. When she was being delivered, she had been injured, and as a result, her right side had not filled out completely like her left side. That was the reason she walked with a limp, and was unable to raise her right arm completely. When she began praising the Lord, it was not but just a few minutes until she began speaking in tongues. When the Lord filled her with the Holy Spirit, He also instantly healed her! Right in front of the church, her entire right side became exactly the same size as her left side! Her right arm was raised to the same level as her left arm!

I don't have to tell you, but the church exploded with praise and worship! The girl had been born and raised in the church. Everyone knew her and what her problem had been. A creative miracle had taken place. That was the result of fasting and prayer. I went to the church the next day to have lunch with the pastor, and there the girl was, running and playing with her friends on the school grounds. That was something she had never been able to do.

I was amazed at what the Lord did in that first meeting. The next revival was in Rialto, California. I prayed for people who had the same condition I had, and when I prayed for them, they were healed. They would come back the next night and testify to their healing. In the meantime, I would sit in the bathtub in hot water during the day just to have relief from the pain. The pain would return, and remain, until I stepped behind the pulpit to preach. Then it would leave, and remain gone, until I finished the altar service. That happened day after day.

I flew from Southern California to Northern California after those two meetings. Just after I arrived at Concord (the third revival location in California), I received word from the fourth church in California, where I was to go for the next meeting, that something had come up, and we would not be able to have the revival. I continued experiencing excruciating pain all during the revival at Concord. It was also during that revival that I received word that the fifth revival I was to preach (which was to be held in Mannford, Oklahoma) was cancelled, due to a tornado striking the church.

I called my doctor on Friday, before I was scheduled to close on Sunday in Concord, and told him that things were not getting better, and that I would have to come home and have the surgery. I booked my flight and flew back to Oklahoma City the following Monday. I couldn't understand why everything was happening the way it was. It seemed strange that my next two revivals would be cancelled at the same time. It was strange that I could pray for others to be healed of the same problem I had, and yet, I could not get my own healing.

I arrived back in Oklahoma City the following Monday and went directly to the doctor's office. When he did the examination, he discovered an anal ulcer in my colon. That is what had been causing all of my pain and severe bleeding. I was taken into surgery the next day. As I lay there recovering, I asked the Lord why all of this was happening to me. He told me that He had been trying to get my attention, but that I would not listen. He reminded me of what He had laid on my heart back in January, about starting a new church in Oklahoma City. He told me that I would not stop and listen to what He had wanted me to do, so He had to get my attention. I hate it that I am so hardheaded!

While I had been in California, Gretnia sold our house and moved to Yukon, Oklahoma. So, when I left the hospital, I was taken to another house, rather than the one we had lived in when I left. A couple of days after I went home, I began running a high fever. I was taken back to the hospital with an infection in the area of my surgery. It was necessary to redo the surgery. I had to spend another five days in the hospital before I could go home. All of this was happening, and I didn't have hospitalization insurance. I was considered uninsurable because of the heart attack I had experienced back in 1980. The Lord had healed me of my heart attack, but the insurance company didn't look at it that way. The hospital cost for my anal ulcer surgery was astronomical.

While I was recovering at home, the Lord continued to talk to me about starting a new church in north Oklahoma City. I had three couples come to visit one night: Bob and Linea Dudley, Charles and Diane Lewellen, and Bill and Laquitta Mash. The women went into another room, and the men stayed in my room so we could talk. Bob and Charles told me that they had been talking, and had wanted to see if I would be interested in starting a new church. I could hardly believe my ears! The Lord had sent men to talk to me, about the very thing which He had been dealing with me about.

I shared with them how the Lord had been dealing with my heart about starting a new church and how I had asked the Lord that if it were His will, that He would have people come to me, and ask me to start the church. It was evident that the Lord had allowed the things in my life to happen to me, just so He could get my attention. Now, He had answered my other prayer. There wasn't a doubt in my mind that He wanted a new church in the north part of Oklahoma City. I was then ready to do what He wanted me to do. My faith was continuing to grow. He was leading me to do something I had never done before.

Chapter Nine
STARTING A NEW CHURCH

In the latter part of May, 1984 the Lord was leading me further into this new adventure of faith. It was exciting. I was being given the privilege of starting a new church, something I felt that the north side of Oklahoma City needed. (There were more than twenty Assemblies of God churches south of I-40 in Oklahoma City, and only six north of I-40.)

Within a few days of coming to visit Gretnia and me, Charles and Diane Lewellen invited a group to their house to discuss the new church. There were twelve adults and seven children present. After our discussion we voted unanimously to start the church. We decided on the name, "Trinity Church." The ball was rolling! We began meeting each week after that. It was wonderful, having the opportunity to get together and worship.

We knew that we had to have a corporation in order to have a church. It did not take but a short period of time to get the church incorporated. We just had to file the papers with the state and pay the fee for the corporation. I met with the A/G District officials to let them know what we wanted to do. We had to have their approval in order to start the church. I knew that they had a meeting scheduled during camp meeting, so we had to start looking for a place to start the church.

I began driving over the north part of Oklahoma City, trying to find a building suitable for the church. Bill Parker, a close friend of mine, called one day and told me that there was a church on the street behind his house that was for sale. He gave me the phone number that was on the sign in front of the church. I called and discovered that it was an Episcopal Church who wanted to sell in order to move to a new location.

Several of us met at the Episcopal Church to see if it would meet our needs. I think all of us fell in love with the church. The location was great for our needs. The church was located at 3025 Center Street, which was right between Sunrise Street and Sunset Street in the Village. It appeared the Lord was working in our behalf.

I met on the first of July with the District Board of the Assemblies of God at their regular meeting at the beginning of camp meeting. We had found a building and the District had approved our request to start Trinity Church. Now, all we needed was for the Episcopal Church to agree to sell to us.

We made an offer to the church and then met at our house to wait and see if they would accept our offer. There were several of us who had fasted the entire day. The phone call finally came and we were told that they had had an interesting meeting. They had begun the discussion about selling the church, and it had appeared that it was not going to pass when suddenly, the entire mood changed and they voted unanimously to sell us the church. The Lord was working in our behalf. Now we had a building. All we had to do was get the money to pay for it.

I went to a banker with whom I had done a great deal of business, and she agreed to loan the money to the church if I could get people to co-sign the note. The people responded beautifully, and we had the money to buy the church. We were able to close the loan quickly and get started in remodeling the platform. The people turned out to get the work done. In fact, there were people who came to help us who did not even attend the church. We remodeled the platform and painted the areas that needed painting. We installed new carpet. When it was finished, it was beautiful.

Our first Sunday was August 5, 1984. There were 143 in attendance. We were amazed at the people who came. We had not requested assistance from the District to start the church because the Lord was providing in every way. We were off and running! The Lord was honoring our faith and obedience to Him. I'll never forget the feeling I had as we began singing in that first service, "All Hail the Power of Jesus Name." The presence of the Lord was especially real in that first service.

There was not a doubt that Trinity was ordained by the Lord. There were a number of people who began attending, who had experienced disappointing things in their previous churches. Trinity became a place where healing could take place in their lives. I told several people who had been deeply involved in other churches, to just sit and relax and allow the Holy Spirit to bring healing, which He did.

We canvassed the entire area around the church. We knocked on doors and invited our neighbors to visit the church, that is, if they did not have a regular church home. Several new people started attending. The attendance that first Sunday was a little deceiving, because there were a number who attended that I knew were members of other churches—they had simply come to see what was happening in our new church.

The church needed a piano, so Gretnia and I brought our Yamaha baby grand piano to the church. We found a Hammond B3 organ located in Muskogee, Oklahoma. The music company delivered the organ to us at no cost. We were greatly blessed to have wonderful musicians. Gretnia played the piano, and Sondie Garner, who lived in Ada at the time, played the organ. Sondie and her husband Gene drove back and forth from Ada every week until we got a regular organist. We will forever be indebted to them. Sadly, Sondie was killed in a car wreck several years ago. The Lord also sent us a drummer and guitar players. We had several talented backup singers as well. Kenny, our son, led the worship. Our worship services were tremendously blessed from the very beginning.

Gretnia became the secretary of the church. We both had regular church hours. I suppose it was because of my experience at Faith Tabernacle, but I felt that a pastor needed to be available in case he was needed. Gretnia and I enjoyed the privilege of working together. That was the first time in our pastoral ministry that we were together, day after day, side by side. When we were at Faith Tabernacle she had been greatly involved in writing and producing our Christmas plays and Easter pageants, but she had not been involved in the day-to-day operation of the church.

Joe and Mark Stevens were a great blessing to the church. They provided a sound board, microphones and speakers, and chairs for the church. Slowly, but surely, we were getting the things that we needed.

We did not have Sunday School when we first started because we did not have the workers necessary to do the job. It didn't take long for the Lord to give us the people we needed though, and then we had the workers to take care of all the classes.

The rest of 1984 was exciting as we began feeling at home in our new church. The platform had been remodeled to accommodate the piano, organ, and other instruments, as well as the backup singers. David and Gayla Collins began attending the church and David made us a beautiful pulpit and communion table, and Gayla began playing the organ when Gene and Sondie Garner could no longer drive back and forth from Ada.

Greg Whitlow, who was Sectional Presbyter at the time, came and set the church in order, which simply meant that he saw to it that we were recognized by the General Council of the Assemblies of God as a sovereign church. My dream of establishing a new church was coming true. The Lord had spoken to my heart about Trinity, and to see it all coming together was wonderful. Tom Greene, who was District Youth Director then, came and spoke for us. It was so meaningful, to have Tom come and preach, because he had received his call into the ministry while I was his pastor at Faith Tabernacle. After all, he was our nephew, and Gretnia and I were extremely proud of him and his family.

We began 1985 with 137 in attendance the first Sunday of the year. We were blessed to have a number of outstanding guests willing to come to our new church. Rozie Rozell, who had been the tenor for the famous Statesmen's Quartet, came to us in February. I had always loved to hear Rozie sing "O, What A Savior." He was a great blessing to our church.

Our first Easter was April 7, 1985. There were 180 in attendance that Sunday morning. What a wonderful day! We started a kid's crusade with "Chief" John McPherson that Sunday night. Since the emphasis was on children, the attendance was not nearly as large as it had been on Sunday morning; however, the attendance grew to 100 by Friday night. Nine children gave their hearts to the Lord during the crusade!

Evangelist Danny Duvall started a revival with us on April 28th. We had a great outpouring of the Holy Spirit during his revival. Danny was engaged to be married, but had not yet bought the ring for his fiancée, when he came to be with us. Our church was very generous in giving to our guests. His offering was a little over $1200 until a man came and gave me a check for another $2500. The man told me he had been tremendously blessed by Danny's ministry and that the Lord had spoken to his heart to give the extra offering. I had been an evangelist long enough to know that when a pastor folded a check and gave it to me saying, "I just wish this could have been for more," the offering was not going to be very good. So, I folded the check and gave it to Danny and said, "You know our church is not very big, I just wish this could have been for more." I asked him to open it and see if it would help him. When he opened the check, he couldn't believe his eyes. The check was for $3700! That wasn't bad for a Sunday through Wednesday! He took the money from that offering and bought Gayla, his fiancée, her engagement ring.

We were blessed to have Rev. Don Brankel with us for Pentecost Sunday, May 26th. Brother Brankel was and is a great Holy Ghost preacher. It touched my heart that these well-known ministers would come to our new church. Brother Brankel could have been in a much larger church if he had wanted.

I believe in having missionaries on a regular basis. Otis Keener was our first missionary. Gary Davidson, missionary to Ireland, was the next to come. It has always been my conviction that we must support our missionaries. We must have a vision to reach the entire world, not just our little world.

Gretnia and I were able to attend the General Council of the Assemblies of God in August. I had scheduled our Vacation Bible School for August 19–23. Eleven children were saved in the VBS! Again, I believe that we must have a well-rounded program for our people. We need something that will be a blessing for everyone.

Kelly Goins, a very talented and dedicated young man came to us in October. His ministry was well received by our people. I later had the privilege of having him on staff with me at Broken Arrow Assembly of God. Today he is a pastor in Tulsa, Oklahoma.

Rev. Dan Betzer, speaker for *Revivaltime,* the national radio broadcast of the Assemblies of God, came to us on November 17th. He was a tremendous blessing to our people. I had had him to come and speak when I was pastor at Faith Tabernacle. Faith Tabernacle was a much larger church than Trinity, but that did not make any difference to Brother Betzer. I will be forever indebted to him for his kindness to us. He came and preached like he was in front of a large congregation.

The church averaged 113 for 1985, the first full year of its existence. There were 43 who gave their hearts to the Lord and 7 who were filled with the Holy Spirit. We were learning to depend more and more on the Lord. Our faith was growing as the Lord continued to meet all of our needs.

We began 1986 with special services on January 19th, with Rev. John G. Hall, renowned teacher on Biblical prophecy. I have always endeavored to have all different kinds of ministry for the people. We must give our people the right kind of teach-ings if we expect them to mature properly. If we give them only one kind of ministry, then they will never know that there are other kinds of ministry available.

I began a series on fasting based on **Isaiah 58:6** which says **"Is not this the fast that I have chosen?"** When I concluded the series, I asked how many would be willing to fast at least one day a week. We had 21 who stated that they would fast one day a week. I divided the 21 into teams of 3, giving us three people, every day of the week who were fasting. We immediately began receiving reports of prayers being answered. When Jesus was asked by His disciples in **Matthew 17:19, " . . . Why could not we cast him (demonic spirit) out?"** Jesus replied in **Matthew 17:21, "Howbeit this kind goeth not out but by prayer and fasting."** If we are going to see miracles in our churches today, we must get back to praying and fasting! The Lord was leading me in my faith life. He had impressed upon my heart the need for fasting. I had to convey that message to the church in order for them to understand the need for fasting.

The attendance on Easter Sunday in 1986 was 172. Gretnia did a special presentation that Sunday morning entitled, "Mary's Song." She had done the same thing when we were at Faith Tabernacle. Kenny, our son, played Jesus, and Gretnia sang the words to him. When she finished, I don't think there was a dry eye in the place.

Our teenagers went to Youth Camp at Turner Falls in June and our children went to Kid's Camp in July. I believe it is important to allow our young people to be involved in as many district functions as possible. Our young people would return from camp on fire for the Lord. I have witnessed a mighty outpouring of the Holy Spirit in all of the churches we have pastored when I would give the youth a chance to give their testimonies after youth camp. I believe in our youth camps!

As I was praying one day, the Lord laid a couple on my heart. I had heard that Harold and Cheryl Price were not really involved in a church. (Harold had been a deacon of mine back at Faith Tabernacle.) I decided I would go and visit them and invite them to Trinity Church. I was warmly received when I went to visit them. We had a great time reminiscing about earlier days. I told them that the Lord had laid them on my heart. I told them that I loved them, and wanted to invite them to church. I was thrilled when they came. It was not long until they were deeply involved in the church. Harold began singing as one of our backup singers. He had always had a wonderful voice. He had been a member of the Midstates, a wonderful singing group that had been with me on previous occasions in the church I had pastored in El Reno.

Cheryl had been raised in a denomination that did not believe in speaking in tongues. I will never forget the Sunday morning I went back to where she was sitting, and asked her if she would like to receive the baptism of the Holy Spirit. She stepped out into the aisle and began worshiping the Lord. It wasn't but just a few minutes, when suddenly, she fell prostrate under the power of the Holy Spirit, speaking in tongues. The Lord had gloriously baptized her with the Holy Spirit. I turned and looked at Harold, who was singing with the backup singers that morning, and he was crying, worshiping the Lord. Harold and Cheryl were a great blessing to the church. They are still a blessing to Gretnia and me.

Trinity was indeed a place where broken lives and wounded spirits could find solace. There was a great deal of love evident in the church. I think many times we are not even aware of all of the blessings we have in a church. It is wonderful to have a body of believers who genuinely care about each other.

I was not even aware of how blessed Gretnia and I were to have our family members in the church. It was wonderful having Kenny, our son, Kathy, our daughter-in-law, and Karmen, Kamber, and Kelly, our granddaughters, in the church. It was wonderful having Tammy, our daughter, my mom, Juanita Deaton, and Gretnia's mom and dad, Thomas and Gurtha Grant, in the church. Charles and Ann Phillips, my aunt and uncle, and

Lois Martin, my aunt, were also with us. Gretnia's sister, Carol, and her husband, Mickey, and their children, Michael, Dustin, and Candace were in the church. Chuck and Brenda Phillips and Cary and Jeanette Phillips, two of my cousins and their wives were with us. Otis Garrison, who was married to my cousin, Charletta, and their two children, Andrew and Amy were with us. Otis became my associate pastor and proved to be a great blessing to us. He worked in Christian Education, and helped by preaching on Wednesdays. We formed a great team. Associates are a great blessing when they are compatible to the pastor. My youngest sister, Janet, and her husband, Kenny, and their two boys, Phillip and Stephen were also a part of Trinity.

Debbie Crawford, our niece, and her son, Christopher attended the church. Debbie began dating Tommy Grayson, who was also attending Trinity with his two children, Michelle and Tommy. Tommy and Debbie asked me to do their wedding after one of our Sunday evening services. They wanted it to be a surprise to the family and the entire church body. I can tell you, it was a surprise! After I had given the invitation and finished the altar service, I asked everyone to stay for a wedding. I then called Tommy and Debbie forward and performed the ceremony. It took everyone by complete surprise. That was the first time I had ever done anything like that. There were a lot of firsts at Trinity!

Sybel and Clifton Clark, charter members of Trinity, said that the Lord had ordained Trinity Church. They felt that the Lord had used us to start the church just for them. They had been members of Faith Tabernacle when Gretnia and I pastored there. There were a number of people who felt the same way about the church.

I will never forget the liberty I had to preach at Trinity, or the wonderful moving of the Holy Spirit in the altars. Service after service, week after week, the Holy Spirit moved in our midst. I hunger to see that kind of moving of the Holy Spirit again.

Starting Trinity Church is an experience I will never forget. Being pastor there for over three years is something I will never forget. The Lord used that period of time to build an even greater faith in me. I know that He is faithful. I know that He supplies all of our needs. I know that He performs miracles. We witnessed many miracles during our time at the church.

The time came in 1987 when I knew the Lord was through with me at Trinity. The General Council of the Assemblies of God was held in Oklahoma City that year. Gretnia, because she was the Women's Ministries representative for Section Nine, had the responsibility of preparing communion for the council's memorial service on Sunday morning of the council. We had to prepare communion for 10,000 people. It was necessary for us to be at the Myriad Convention Center at 6:00 A.M. that morning in order to get the things ready. We had a wonderful group of people from other churches that came and helped us. Without them we could never have made it.

I scheduled Don Brankel to speak for us on the Sunday morning of council. John Starnes was to be our special musical guest. We had 205 in attendance that Sunday morning. That was the largest number we had had in the three-plus years since we had been in existence. Even the excitement of that great day could not diminish the feeling I had that the Lord was through with me though. I could not understand why He wanted me to leave, but I have never questioned His will for my life. I didn't know what He had in store for us. I was endeavoring to walk by faith, just as I have always done. I have never worried about what other people may think about the decisions I make for my life. I am endeavoring to please Him. He is the One before whom I will stand one day and give an account of my life. I want to hear Him say, "Well done, thou good and faithful servant."

September 13, 1987 was our last Sunday at Trinity Church. I preached that morning on the subject, "He Must Increase, I Must Decrease." One chapter was closing for Gretnia and me, but He was getting ready to open another chapter.

Chapter Ten
JOURNEY TO BRIGHTMOOR TABERNACLE

When Gretnia and I left Trinity Church we went back on the evangelistic field. I have always had an excitement in preaching revivals. I love seeing the many that come to know the Lord as their Savior. I love praying for people to receive the baptism of the Holy Spirit. I rejoice in seeing the many who receive their miracle of healing. The Lord has always been good to me in allowing me to be where people's faith would touch the Lord. I have always seen many miracles in our revivals.

In the first part of 1988 Gretnia and I received an invitation from Spud DeMent, missionary to Kenya, East Africa, to come to Nairobi, East Africa to preach crusades and help establish a new work in Thika, a village of 60,000, where there was not a church. We were excited at the opportunity and told Spud that we would come if we could raise the money. I felt that the Lord would supply the need for us to go. I knew that the missionaries could not help pay any of the cost because that was not in their budget. We needed the money for everything we would do while there, plus the money for the flights. The total cost was going to be about $7500. The date was set and plans were made for us to go.

When we got to within six weeks of our departure, I had not been able to raise any of our money. I panicked. I called Spud and told him what was happening. He told me to wait another week and see if the Lord would not supply our need. If we did not get the money, then he would understand, and he would cancel the meetings. I was to call him back and let him know for sure. I was in a revival in Liberty, Texas at the time. I had shared with the pastor about the opportunity I had to go to Africa, and he shared with me that he would pray with me that the Lord would supply our needs.

I closed the revival on Wednesday night and got up the next morning to load our van to go to the next meeting. When I walked out of the motel room to load the van, I saw a business card under my windshield wiper. I looked at the card and saw that there was a note on the back of it. The note told me to stop by the office of the man who had given me the card. When Gretnia and I stopped by the office, the man told me that he had heard that we wanted to go to Africa, and that the Lord had spoken to him to pay for our flights. He asked me if I knew how much the flights would cost. I told him the amount, and he gave me a check for our flights. Praise the Lord! The Lord had met a very great need. That was a great boost for my faith! The pastor took Gretnia and me into Houston, and we got our passports and the shots needed for the trip. I called Spud and told him the Lord was working and we would be there.

We drove from Houston to Tucson, Arizona where Rev. Jim Brankel was pastor. Brother Brankel took a special offering for our trip to Africa. The money was beginning to come in. By the time we headed back to Oklahoma City, we were still $1000 short of the money we needed. We stopped by a restaurant owned by some friends of ours in Clinton, Oklahoma to get something to eat on the way home. When we started to leave, Barbara Clark, the owner, gave us an envelope, and told us that the Lord had spoken to her to give us an offering. When we opened the envelope, there were ten $100 bills in it. That was the exact amount we needed to pay for the rest of the trip. The Lord had supplied our every need! Our faith had been boosted again! If He opens a door for you, He will supply your every need!

Gretnia's sister, Laquitta, and her husband, Bill Mash went with us to Africa. They proved to be a real blessing. After the crusade was over in Thika, there had been enough converts that a new church was opened. Bill made all of the pews for the new church and built a beautiful pulpit for the new pastor. The new pastor was graduating from the East Africa School of Theology. He also served as my interpreter for the crusade.

At the end of the service one evening, after I had given the invitation and prayed for the needs of the people, I felt impressed to give another invitation. When I asked if there were others who wanted to respond to the invitation to come forward, I noticed an older man, who had been standing under some trees, step out and begin moving forward. When he got closer to the platform, Martin, the young preacher, turned to me and cried, "That's my uncle. I didn't know he was here. I am the only one in my family who knows the Lord. My family disowned me when I became a Christian." He jumped off the platform and began running to his uncle. He threw his arms around him and began praying for him. When his uncle had stepped out, there were a number of others who followed him to the altar. There was tremendous rejoicing that night as many more gave their hearts to the Lord.

In October we were in revival in Tomball, Texas when I received a phone call from Rev. Thomas Trask, current General Superintendent of the Assemblies of God. He told me that he had been asked to go to Springfield, Missouri to become General Treasurer of the Assemblies of God, and wanted to know if I was interested in pastoring again. He told me that Rev. Don Brankel, who had been in revival with him at Brightmoor Tabernacle in Southfield, Michigan, a suburb of Detroit, where he had been pastor, had recommended me to him.

I must admit that I was amazed that he would call me. I told him that I had not been thinking about being a pastor again, but that I would pray about it and let him know. I did not know anything about Brightmoor Tabernacle, even though I would find out later that it was one of the great churches in the movement, but I had an excitement in my heart about what Brother Trask had asked. I talked it over with Gretnia and told her I was going to the church to pray. The more I prayed, the greater the excitement became. I felt that the Lord wanted me to pursue the opportunity.

I called Brother Trask back the next day and told him how I was feeling. He told me that the church wanted to send a pulpit committee to hear me preach the following Sunday. I had told him I would be starting a revival at Parkdale Assembly of God in Beaumont, Texas. I knew that even though a pulpit committee was coming to hear me preach, I could not change the message the Lord had already given me for the church.

The following Sunday morning, two distinguishing looking gentlemen: one, an F.B.I. agent, and the other, a leading engineer with the Lincoln division of Ford Motor Company, were in the service. I did not speak to them, or they with me. I preached a simple message entitled, "Can There Be A Spiritual Resurrection?" Four people gave their hearts to the Lord and three were filled with the Holy Spirit. The men left and flew back to Detroit.

Brother Trask called me the following Tuesday morning, after the board had met on Monday night, and extended an invitation for me to come to Brightmoor Tabernacle and meet with the board for an interview the following Saturday, and then preach their three services on Sunday.

Gretnia and I both felt an excitement as we flew into Detroit. We were met at the airport by one of the associates. After he picked us up, he drove us around and showed us the church and surrounding community. We could not believe the size of Brightmoor Tabernacle. The church seated 2700. They were averaging 1742 in attendance. We discovered that there had only been two pastors in the history of the church: Bond Bowman and Thomas Trask. I remember thinking, *Lord, is this really happening? A boy from Healdton, Oklahoma being interviewed by the board of one of the greatest churches in the Assemblies of*

God? It was overwhelming to me! Yet, I had a perfect peace in my heart that this was the perfect will of God for our lives. Faith was leading us in this new experience.

I met with the board that evening and preached the three services on Sunday. Sunday morning I preached the message, "I Saw the Lord," in both services. I couldn't believe my eyes as 68 people responded to the altar calls. Sunday night I preached the message, "Heaven's Rain." Twelve more responded to the invitation for salvation and fourteen were filled with the Holy Ghost. It had truly been a tremendous day! The board met and invited us to come back on November 20th as candidates for their pastor. I couldn't explain what I was feeling inside. I just knew, that I knew, that we would be voted in as pastor. My faith was working. **Hebrews 11:1** says **"Now faith is the substance of things hoped for, the evidence of things not seen."** We continued preaching revivals the next month, but I could hardly wait to go back to Brightmoor. I stayed on my face and prayed and prayed that the Lord's perfect will would be done in our lives. It was in His hands!

When we flew back to the church, the board set up a social gathering where the congregation could come and meet us and ask questions. It gave us a chance to meet the people. The people were delightful.

November 20, 1988 finally arrived. That Sunday morning I preached the message, "A Little Farther." Twenty-six people responded to the invitation in the two services. Sunday night I preached, "Behold, A Greater Than Solomon is Here." Ten more responded to the invitation. Gretnia and I then went back to Brother Trask's office to wait for the vote. Brother Trask had asked what kind of percentage I wanted; to let me know that it was the Lord's will for us to be elected. I told him I had asked the Lord for at least 80% of the vote. When he came to get us, he said, "Congratulations, you are the new pastors of Brightmoor Tabernacle. You received 91% of the vote." Amazingly, that was the exact percentage we received when we were voted in at Faith Tabernacle! He then took us into the auditorium. When we walked in, the congregation gave us a standing ovation. He then introduced us as the new pastors of the church. It was overwhelming! Gretnia and I were the pastors of Brightmoor Tabernacle! I could have sung, "We've come this far by faith, leaning on the Lord . . ."

I met with the board after Gretnia and I had received all the congratulations from the people. It was an exciting time in our lives. When I met with the board, they told me that we had not discussed a salary. I told them that I had done that on purpose. I told them I felt that they would take care of their pastor. They then told me that I was the only candidate who had done that. They were very generous in what they gave me. It was decided that we would assume the responsibility of the church on the first Sunday of 1989.

Lou Focht, and his wife Betty, took us out after the services. Lou was the vice-chairman of the board. He had been one of the two men who had come to Beaumont, Texas to hear me preach. They became some of our best friends, and still are to this day.

After we got back to the hotel, we started calling all of our family members and friends, to let them know what had happened. It was a dream come true! We had an exciting Christmas that year, knowing we were going to Brightmoor Tabernacle.

Brother Trask had told me when we took the church, that he felt the church was ready for revival. I found that to be true when we arrived. From the very first service through the next eighteen months, people were saved and filled with the Holy Spirit in every service.

I began our new ministry at Brightmoor by preaching on the baptism of the Holy Spirit. In the very first service, five were saved and ten were filled with the Holy Spirit. For the next three consecutive weeks I preached on "The Benefit of Speaking in Other Tongues." There were 19 saved and 69 who received the baptism of the Holy Spirit in those services. The Lord was setting the mood for a Pentecostal revival in Brightmoor.

I had not been at Brightmoor very long when the Lord impressed upon my heart the need of preaching on "Praising the Lord." I began the series on Sunday evenings. I preached nineteen weeks on the subject. As I was concluding the first sermon, I was telling how Solomon wanted the presence of the Lord to come as he was dedicating the temple. I told them Solomon had a father who knew how to praise the Lord. David would orchestrate praises. He would call for the trumpeters to play their trumpets. He would call for the cymbal players to play their cymbals. He would call for the singers to sing praises. For those who could not sing or play, he would call for shouters to shout praises. I then asked our trumpet players to come back to the platform. I asked our drummer to come back, but I told him I just wanted him to play the cymbals. I asked our choir to return to the platform. Then I asked if there were any shouters in Brightmoor. There were a number of hands that went up. I asked all of them to come to the platform. I asked our minister of music to lead the singers, players, and shouters in praising the Lord. The Holy Spirit began moving in a tremendous way as people began praising the Lord.

After a period of time of worship, I asked my minister of music to give me an E-flat chord on the piano. I did not say anything about a Jericho march. I did not give any instructions on how to have a Jericho march. I didn't even know if the church knew what a Jericho march was. I began singing, "When the Saints Go Marching in." Brightmoor had six sections on the bottom floor. When we began singing, spontaneously and simultaneously, the people in each of the sections began marching around their sections. There were six Jericho marches going on at the same time. All heaven was coming down in the sanctuary. After quite some time of worship, I asked how many needed healing. I told the people to line up around the sanctuary if they needed healing. There were more than 350 people who lined up for prayer. When I began praying for the people, they were slain under the power of God, all over the sanctuary. Many of the people I never touched. The Holy Spirit simply took over. We were experiencing a sovereign move of the Holy Spirit!

I felt the need of preaching on "Fasting." I started the series one Sunday morning and preached nine messages beginning with **Isaiah 58:6** which says **"Is not this the fast that I have chosen? To loose the bands of wickedness, to undo the heavy burdens, and to let the oppressed go free, and that ye break every yoke?"** When the disciples had been unable to cast the demonic spirit out of the young man in **Matthew 17,** they asked the Lord "Why?" The Lord answered them in **verse 21, "Howbeit this kind goeth not out but by prayer and fasting. "** We need fasting with our prayers to enable us to do what they could not do. At the end of the nine-week series I asked how many would be willing to fast one day a week? 210 people raised their hands saying that they would fast. I divided those 210 up into seven teams of 30. That gave us 30 people, fasting and praying, every day for the needs of our people to be met. I had my secretary prepare a list of the prayer requests that we received each week. Those lists were handed out at the end of the Sunday evening service. Immediately, we began receiving reports of miracles.

One couple had a baby born with a water head. The baby was scheduled for surgery on Monday morning. Sunday night they asked us to pray for a miracle for their baby. They got up on Monday morning to take the baby in for surgery, but the baby's head was absolutely normal! The Lord had performed a miracle! **"Howbeit this kind goeth not out but by prayer and fasting!"**

One of our ladies worked in the Michigan Medical Center in Lansing. She worked with a nurse who was from the Philippines. The nurse had an aneurysm in her brain and was scheduled for surgery. The night before her surgery, she came to Brightmoor for prayer. The lady from our church had told her that the Lord was performing miracles, and wanted her to come to church before she had surgery. The nurse told me that she had never been in a Pentecostal church before. I asked her if she really believed that the Lord could heal her. She informed me that she did believe. I anointed both sides of her head with oil and prayed for her. She said she felt a different sensation when I prayed. She told me her head suddenly became very light and she felt like she was floating, and she could not feel the pain in her head anymore. She told me that she felt completely different. When she checked into the hospital the next morning, she informed her doctor that she wanted another MRI done before she would allow them to do the surgery. When they did the MRI, they discovered that the aneurysm was gone! The Lord had performed another miracle. Miracles were becoming commonplace in our services. There's not a doubt in my mind that the Lord was honoring our fasting and praying. It will still work today!

We began receiving requests for prayer from all over the United States. The word was spreading that the Lord was answering prayer at Brightmoor Tabernacle. I know that it was because of our fasting and prayer. In fact, I have a folder, filled with documented reports of healing. I always encouraged the people for whom we prayed, to go back to their doctor for verification. When the Lord heals us, we will stand the test of doctor's examinations.

One family had a baby born without the thalamus and corpus callosum, two parts of its brain. After we had prayed and anointed a handkerchief, which was placed on the baby's head, the baby was taken back to the neurosurgeon for further tests. EKG's and CAT scans were done. The doctor came out; looking puzzled, and informed the parents that there was no evidence of missing brain parts. The Lord had performed a creative miracle.

One of the men in the church had been born with a congenital heart problem; he had a hole in his heart. At fourteen he had had a heart attack and could no longer play baseball. He had

had a heart operation in 1986 to repair his problem, but after being home just a few days, he suffered a stroke which left his left side partially paralyzed. His heart then began a rapid heartbeat of 160 beats a minute. He was given a shock treatment, as well as medication, at the time, to get his heartbeat back to normal. However, the problem never subsided and three years later, despite taking medication, he was still suffering with an irregular heartbeat. When he would get up in the morning, his heart would go into a rapid heartbeat for a minute or so and then it would settle back down to normal again. He had become very depressed because the doctors couldn't seem to get rid of his problem. I called for people who needed prayer for healing to come forward one Sunday morning and he responded. The Lord healed him instantly that morning! His heartbeat was restored to normal and no longer did he need his medication. After his healing, he sent his doctors a letter telling them they did not have to worry about a lawsuit because the Lord had healed him. (He sent a copy of the same letter to me.)

I had an associate whose father was on vacation in Florida. While in Florida, he was taken to the hospital, believed to have had a heart attack. The doctors performed an ultrasound examination and gave the following report: "The abdominal aorta was scanned with the patient in a supine and right lateral decubitus positions. There is a large, fusiformed aneurysm measuring, at it largest diameter, 5.0 cm. The walls of the aorta are calcified. There is extensive, calcified thrombus within the aneurysm. The common iliac arteries are dilated." We were called at the church and informed of his condition. We went to prayer immediately. He was brought back to Michigan where he underwent an echocardiogram by other doctors. This was their report: "Normal appearing gall bladder, biliary tree, liver, spleen, aorta, pancreas and both kidneys are seen. **No evidence of aneurysm!**" The Lord had performed a miracle.

Since I was the new pastor at the church it seemed that everyone wanted to see me. As a result, I found myself scheduled all day with little time to study and pray, as had been my custom. I called my secretary into my office and told her that I would not be taking any appointments until after lunch each day. I told her that I was giving the Lord the first part of every day. If I expected Him to bless and anoint my ministry, then I must put Him first. I began a new schedule immediately. When I arrived at the church, which was about 8:30 each morning, I went into the sanctuary to pray. I would pray at least one hour before I went back into my office. I would then read my Bible and start studying for my messages. I preached at least four different messages each week. Besides our Sunday services, we had a Tuesday service at which I spoke, and the Wednesday evening service. I also had a daily radio broadcast, "God's Word for Today," on a local station. Our eleven o'clock Sunday morning service was also live on radio. The schedule kept me jumping.

When I was being interviewed for the job, I was told that the entire staff had submitted their resignations. I told the board that I would accept the resignations, but I would not act on them until I had been there for at least three months. I told the board that I did not have a staff to bring with me, and I wanted to see if the current staff could work with me, and I with them. The three-month period would give us time to adjust to each other. At the end of that three-month period, I asked all ten of the staff members to remain on staff and they all agreed to stay. Brother Trask had done a wonderful job in getting a very sufficient staff.

I had not been at the church very long when I started having "anointing services," in our Sunday morning worship services. I asked all of the staff and board members to come forward, stand across the front of the church, and anoint the people who had needs in their lives. We began seeing people saved, filled with the Holy Spirit, and healed in those anointing services. The Lord was meeting the needs of His people.

Our worship was absolutely heavenly. There was a beautiful blend of the old songs and the new choruses. I can remember standing, with my eyes closed, and thinking, this must be what heaven is going to be like. We had a full orchestra and choir that ministered in the services. It was necessary to have a water baptismal service at the beginning of every Sunday evening service because so many people were being saved each week.

The church was growing. On Easter Sunday, we had over 2400 in attendance. There were more than 2700 on Mother's Day. Those were special days when many visitors attended the services. It was undeniable that the Lord was moving in a special way.

John G. Hall was our first evangelist. His ministry on prophecy was a great blessing to the church. He had been there on previous occasions. Don Brankel came for revival, followed by Danny Duvall. The people were excited about what the Lord was doing.

By the end of the first year we had lost about one-fourth of the congregation. They had left and began attending Highland Park Baptist Church and Ward Presbyterian Church. Even though we had that many to leave, the Lord gave us an overall increase in our attendance. He had more than replaced the ones who left. The church had increased from an average of 1742 to 1992. That placed Brightmoor Tabernacle as the ninth largest church in the Assemblies of God according to the annual report that year.

I have seen what happened at Brightmoor, happen in other churches. When you start preaching on the baptism of the Holy Spirit, it will separate those who don't want the moving of the Holy Spirit, from those who do want the moving of the Spirit. There are many people attending our churches today who are not comfortable with the moving of the Holy Spirit. They enjoy our music and worship, but do not see the need of speaking in tongues. They can be Pentecostal in name, but not in experience. The thing that has made our Assemblies of God what it is, is the moving and demonstration of the Holy Spirit in our services.

God has given us something wonderful in Pentecost! It was through the power and the anointing of the Holy Spirit that our churches were birthed! It was through the power and the anointing of the Holy Spirit that our churches experienced growth! It was through the power and the anointing of the Holy Spirit that our early-day preachers overcame the many obstacles and resistance to the Pentecostal message! They endured rotten eggs and tomatoes, and threats to their lives! The yoke was destroyed because of the anointing of the Holy Spirit! I don't want to ever forget our heritage!

I don't know of anytime in my life when I felt as much liberty to preach as I did at Brightmoor. There was an excitement in my heart every time I stood before that congregation. The words simply flowed. The thoughts were always there. I didn't have to search for something to say. Every service was greatly blessed and anointed by the Holy Spirit. As I said earlier, there was not one service but what people were saved and filled with the Holy Spirit. The tithes increased dramatically that first year. Missions giving increased by $100,000. It was beyond my comprehension what the Lord was doing.

I invited Bill and Retha Shell to come to Brightmoor to serve as my Business Administrators. (Bill had been my Business Administrator and Christian Education Director while I was at Faith Tabernacle in Oklahoma City, Oklahoma.) They were a great blessing to me in helping operate the church. I will never forget their commitment and dedication during the transitional time at Brightmoor. Brother Shell was always a help to me. He was always easy-going and deliberate in his thinking and actions, whereas I was always more aggressive. He helped to provide the balance that I needed. Retha was an outstanding accountant. She was invaluable in our bookkeeping department. I always knew that all of the reports were going to be accurate if she had anything to do with them. She was a perfectionist when it came to those things.

We entered into the new year of 1990 on a high. The Lord had blessed Brightmoor beyond measure. More than 1000 had been saved in 1989. Those were the ones who had given us their names and addresses. We followed up on every one of them. I sent a letter to everyone by Tuesday, following his or her conversion. They were contacted by a staff member and visited by our cell group leaders. All of them did not stay at Brightmoor. Many went to other churches closer to where they lived. We had over 300 filled with the Holy Spirit in 1989. We had experienced one year of Holy Ghost revival!

When the Lord is moving, as He had been doing in the church, the devil does not like it. I discovered that there were some in the church who didn't like what the Lord was doing. They were prominent, powerful people who had been in the church a long time. They felt that my ministry was attracting the wrong kind of people to the church. They were afraid that Brightmoor was changing, and, it was. It didn't matter how much the church had grown, or that the offerings had increased, or that the missions giving had increased. It didn't matter that people were being saved and filled with the Holy Spirit in every service. They just didn't want the changes that were occurring.

I began feeling in my prayer times that something was happening. I couldn't put my finger on it at first. Everyday I began praying the words in **Ephesians 6:12: "For we wrestle not against flesh and blood, but against principalities, against powers, against the rulers of darkness of this world, against spiritual wickedness in high places."** It was not long before I found out what was happening.

In a board meeting one of the deacons informed me that he did not think I was the right person for the job of pastor. You could have heard a pin drop. The majority of the board was in shock, just as I was. The deacon told me that my ministry was attracting the wrong kind of people to the church. That meeting began a series of several months of meetings just like it. There were a couple of deacons who were determined to get rid of me.

In the midst of all the turmoil, the Lord was still moving in every service. I know that the majority of the church was not even aware of what was happening. It would not be of any benefit to go into all the details of what was happening. We cannot go back and change anything that happened. We just have to leave it all in the hands of the Lord.

The climax came in June of 1990. The two deacons who wanted to get rid of me had been talking to a number of the people in the church, expressing their feelings. That was not permitted, according to the constitution and by-laws of Brightmoor Tabernacle. The majority of the deacons who were still standing by my side and I, decided to call the two deacons in for a meeting, and give them a chance to resign. If they did not resign, we would then call a special business meeting for the Sunday evening service, and present to the church body what was happening, and vote on them.

The Saturday evening before we were to meet on Sunday morning, I received a phone call from a district official, asking what was happening. I told him we were having a board meeting the next morning. He asked if he could be present. I told him that I didn't think it would be necessary for him to be there because we were just conducting church business. He then told me that he wanted to meet with me at the church before our board meeting the next morning. I suddenly had a sick feeling in the pit of my stomach. He had already talked to me (in an earlier meeting) about resigning, saying it was in the best interest of the church. He told me that the church was changing and that he did not want that to happen. In fact, I had been offered a generous severance package if I would resign. When I got off the phone with the district official that night, I told Gretnia that we had lost the pastorate. I didn't know what was happening, but I knew that something was about to happen. The Michigan District had a resolution in place declaring that if a church were deemed to be in trouble, the district could take that church under district supervision. It was evident that that was what was happening.

I was unable to sleep that night. I prayed and prayed until about 5:30 A.M. I then called Armon Newburn, my former district superintendent in Oklahoma, told him what was happening, and asked his advice. He told me that he thought I could win the battle that morning, but questioned whether I could win the war. He then asked how my blood pressure was doing, knowing that I had experienced a major heart attack back in 1980. I told him it had gotten extremely high. He told me that he would really like to be able to play some more golf with me and that he would be praying for me.

The next morning, district officials were at the church at 7:00 A.M. I told them that I would resign if that is what they were wanting. They accepted my resignation, and we went into the board meeting. I told the board what was happening. I told them that I had submitted my resignation and that we would not be discussing the two board members as we had planned. I had to leave after several minutes of discussion because I had to preach our first service which started at 8:30 A.M. I walked out of that board meeting with the heaviest feeling I can ever recall. I felt as though my world was crashing around me.

After I left the board meeting, all of the board members were asked to resign, effective immediately. Brightmoor Tabernacle, one of the greatest churches in the Assemblies of God, had been placed under district supervision! During the meeting (after I had left) one of the board members asked if I had resigned under pressure. He was told that I had.

The district officials and the board came into the service while it was in progress. I preached the message that the Lord had laid on my heart for service that morning, "My God Shall Supply All Your Needs." At the conclusion of the message, I resigned. My heart was breaking! I knew that it was not God's will! One of the officials then came to the pulpit and told the church that all of the board had resigned. He then told the church that he wanted the church to pray for Gretnia and me. He asked the board members and their wives to come forward to pray for us. The two board members who had been opposed to us were the first ones to respond. When they laid their hands on Gretnia and me, Gretnia began crying, "Oh, my God, no, no!" She collapsed, and I picked her up in my arms and carried her out while she was crying. We were taken into my office, where a doctor from the church, came and ministered to us. We were unable to go back to the church for the evening service.

The following Sunday morning, the district officials came to talk to the church. One of the officials was asked if there were any charges against me. He was asked if I had done anything wrong. He informed them that I had done nothing wrong, and that there were no charges against me. Many people got up and left the church that morning. It is sad what has happened to the church since that time. The income dropped almost one million dollars the first year. The crowd dropped considerably. It continued to drop over the next several years, until the church no longer had Sunday School and finally, no Sunday evening services.

You may wonder why I would share something like this. The reason I have, is to let you know that your faith will be tested in many different ways. The experience at Brightmoor Tabernacle was one of the greatest tests of my faith. I can share with you today that the Lord has brought Gretnia and me through. Our faith was tested, and I believe, strengthened, because of what happened. I can tell you that the Lord is faithful! I can tell you that He has supplied all of our needs! I wouldn't want to go through something like that again, but I learned a great deal through that experience.

In the 18 months we were at Brightmoor, there were over 1400 saved, more than 400 filled with the Holy Ghost, and numerous miracles of healing. Witnessing those miracles built our faith. The Lord was wonderful to Gretnia and me to allow us the privilege of going to such a great church. We will remember the many good times. We met some of the most wonderful people in the world while we were there. Many of them are still our friends today. As I stated earlier, we cannot go back and change anything. We must keep pressing towards the mark for the prize of the high calling. We must stay faithful. We must keep watching and waiting for the soon return of the Lord.

What I have shared is in no way to place blame on anyone. We all do the best we can under the circumstances. I love everyone who was involved and pray for them. After all, we are all going to spend eternity together one day. We just have to keep living and walking by faith!

Chapter Eleven
THE JOURNEY CONTINUES

When Gretnia and I left Brightmoor Tabernacle, we moved back to Oklahoma City. We were at a loss as to what was happening. We had felt when we moved to Michigan, that we would be there the rest of our lives. That had not happened! We discovered that when man interferes with God's perfect will, that the Lord has a progressive will, which means that God's will changes as circumstances change in our lives.

Around this time I was reminded of a sermon I had heard Gene Jackson, who became the Superintendent of the Tennessee District Council of the Assemblies of God, preach entitled, "Trouble Isn't Trouble." He had used **James 1:2, "My brethren, count it all joy when ye fall into divers temptations,"** as his text. He said you must count it all joy in the triumphs *and* in the trials of your life. There are times, known only to Him, when God says to the servant, "No, we're not going to do it the way you want to do it." It is important that we understand that as a servant, our loyalty is to Him, regardless of our circumstances. He said that there are times when God's people go through trials, but that troubles aren't really troubles, if they cause you to depend upon the Lord. Gretnia and I were at the place in our lives where we were depending upon Him completely.

Dan Sheaffer, the pastor of Crossroads Cathedral and a very close friend of ours, immediately invited Gretnia and me to minister in his great church. Crossroads was more than twice as large as Brightmoor Tabernacle. Dan was a great blessing to us at that time.

Gloria Farjardo, pastor of Cathedral of the Palms in Corpus Christi, Texas, called and invited me to come for a revival meeting in September. It had been three months since I had preached. I was wondering if I would still feel the anointing of the Holy Spirit. When I stood to preach in the first service of that revival, the Holy Spirit spoke to my heart and said, "I have not lifted my anointing from you. You will continue to feel my presence and have my anointing." I cannot explain what I felt in that moment! I just knew that the Lord was with us! In that ten-day revival, 86 were saved and 96 received the baptism of the Holy Spirit according to Gloria's report. An exciting new chapter had begun in our lives. The Lord began opening doors for revivals all over the United States.

Gretnia and I were seeing as many as 500 saved and 600 filled with the Holy Spirit each year. We were witnessing miracles of healing in our revivals. In a revival at Sunset Chapel in Miami, Florida, a woman who had been blind since birth was instantly healed and received her sight. She had come forward, night after night for prayer, and nothing had happened. The revival was extended because we were experiencing such a move of the Holy Spirit. On the last night, after most of the congregation had left, she came forward again for prayer. That time when I prayed for her healing, she began crying, "I can see! I can see!" I was the first person she ever saw. The Lord had instantly healed her and given her sight after forty two years. I believe the Lord had been building her faith in all of the other services and culminated it with complete healing for her eyes.

In a revival at First Assembly of God in Gallup, New Mexico, a woman who was a deaf mute came forward to seek the baptism of the Holy Spirit. While I was praying for her, suddenly she burst out speaking in tongues. Up until that time she had been unable to speak, but when she was baptized in the Holy Spirit, her tongue was loosed and she began speaking in a heavenly language! Her first spoken words were those inspired by the Holy Spirit!

In Venice, Florida, a 91-year-old man with rheumatoid arthritis was instantly healed and began dancing in the Spirit, back and forth across the front of the church. At the same time he was healed, he was filled with the Holy Spirit and began speaking in tongues. It all happened the night a pastor from a denomination which did not believe in modern-day miracles, or speaking in tongues, was in the service. There was nothing the pastor could do or say except give praise to the Lord for what he had witnessed.

At First Assembly of God in Byesville, Ohio, an elderly lady who had been blind for two years due to an irreversible eye condition and who the doctors said would never see again was instantly healed and received her sight.

The Lord then began opening doors for me to preach district meetings. I had been invited to preach the Wyoming District Camp Meeting in 1989, while I was pastor at Brightmoor Tabernacle. I was invited to preach the Oklahoma District Men's Retreat in 1991. I was in a revival in California when I received a phone call from Rev. Robert Crabtree, District Superintendent of the Ohio District, asking me to preach their District Camp Meeting in 1993. In 1994, Rev. Manuel Shoults, Superintendent of the Northern Missouri District at the time, asked me to preach their District Council and District Camp Meeting. I was having difficulty believing all of the doors the Lord was opening. In 1996, Rev. Robert Slaton, Superintendent of the West Texas District, asked me to preach their District Camp Meeting. In 1999, Rev. Howard Burroughs, District Superintendent of the South Texas District, at the time, invited me to preach their District Camp Meeting. I was invited to preach the General Council of the Assemblies of God in Malawi, East Africa in 2000.

In 1996 Gretnia and I were voted in as pastors in Broken Arrow, Oklahoma. We spent over two years there. We praise the

Lord for the fruitful ministry He gave us. The church grew with many being saved and filled with the Holy Spirit.

I began writing a book, "What Is Pentecost Really Like?" in January of 2002. In March of 2002 we were voted in as pastors in Britton, Oklahoma where we spent a year and a half. We felt the Lord had sent us there to do a specific work and when that was done, He released us. My book was published in May of 2003. In September, Gretnia and I were privileged to be interviewed on Daystar T.V. about the book. I received numerous contacts from people wanting the book. Being on Daystar was a blessing to us. I am excited about seeing the book being used as a teaching tool in many of our churches. I put questions after each chapter in the book so that it could be used as a study book. The book was later republished by Tate Publishing Company in Mustang, Oklahoma. They have done a wonderful job in getting the book out into book stores.

2004 began with us back on the evangelistic field. We were invited to speak at Springfield Christian Center in Mooresville, Indiana in February. The pastor, Mark Wright, had arranged for us to be interviewed about my new book on TBN in Indianapolis on February 6th, just before our revival began. There were 4 saved and 48 filled with the Holy Spirit in the revival in his church. We were invited to appear on *The Harvest Show* on the LESEA network on February 12th in South Bend, Indiana. I was interviewed again about my new book. The Lord was opening doors for me, not only for revivals, but also for my book.

I then began writing this book, "Faith Can Move Mountains." The Lord had dealt with me about writing this book back in 1983 when I was preaching a revival in St. Louis, Missouri. I started writing notes down at that time. The pages were turning yellow because it had been so long since I started. I am truly excited about my new book. It is actually an autobiography of mine and Gretnia's lives.

Our revivals continued, taking us to Miami, Florida; Miami, Oklahoma; Lindsay, Oklahoma; Blackwell, Oklahoma;

Newcastle, Tulsa, and Elk City, Oklahoma; Texarkana, Arkansas; and Muskogee, Oklahoma.

Mark and Susie Purkey invited Gretnia and me to go to Italy with them in June. In fact, they paid our way! What a tremendous blessing! We could never thank them enough. There were 21 of us on the trip. We had tremendous services, with a number of people being filled with the Holy Spirit.

We continued in revivals into the month of August. This has been a tremendous year so far. I have completed my second book now and am looking forward to what the Lord has in store for us.

Gretnia went back to Real Estate School and got her real estate license again. She had had them before, but let them lapse when we moved to Michigan. She passed the test on her first try. I am real proud of her.

We have had an exciting journey. I look back to where we started, and see where we are today, and I have to admit, I am amazed. The Lord has led us to so many wonderful places and has blessed us in so many ways. The journey of faith is always exciting! You can't see where you are going, except by faith. I can testify that we have seen many mountains moved. I can testify that we have witnessed many miracles, brought about by faith. I wouldn't take anything for our journey because I know that it isn't finished yet. **FAITH IS STILL MOVING MOUNTAINS!**

CONCLUSION

I have shared with you what the Lord has done in my life from a humble beginning to the present time. I have been blessed beyond measure. I have had an exciting journey of faith. However, what I have experienced can happen to anyone who will dare take his or her own walk of faith.

The first step in your walk of faith is **your commitment to the Lord.** The walk of faith begins with the surrender of your life to the Lord. You cannot take the walk if you never start the journey. **Amos 3:3** asks, **"Can two walk together, except they be agreed?"** You must agree with the Lord on the starting place, as well as the journey you will take. That journey is revealed one day at a time. Ask the Lord to come into your heart and to forgive you of all of your sins. **1 John 1:9** states, **"If we confess our sins, he is faithful and just to forgive us our sins, and to cleanse us from all unrighteousness."** The emphasis is on the word, **"all."** It does not matter what you may have done in your life, the Lord will forgive you of **"all"** your sins. Just think about it: **2 Corinthians 5:12** says **"Therefore if any man be in Christ, he is a new creature: old things are passed away; behold, all things are become new."** When you make a commitment to the Lord of your life, you are starting a new journey. Faith has started!

The second step in your walk of faith is **building your faith through God's Word.** According to **Romans 12:3, " . . . God hath dealt to every man the measure of faith."** It is up to us how much faith we receive. God has given us the source!

Romans 10:17 says **"So then faith cometh by hearing, and hearing by the word of God."** You can have just as much faith as you want. It is developed slowly. The development of your faith depends upon how much time you spend in God's Word.

Faith is to become our life! There is a role we have to play. I want us to look at our part in this **"faith"** life. I don't want to go so fast in this that it runs off before it soaks in!

I want you to look at **Hebrews 3:1** which says, **"Wherefore, holy brethren, partakers of the heavenly calling, *consider* the Apostle and High Priest of our *profession*, Christ Jesus."** It would do us good to just pause for a moment and practice what this verse says—" . . . **consider** the Apostle and High Priest of our **profession**, Christ Jesus"—because He is right where you are at this very moment!

Hold your arms out for a moment. Now look at your hands. Do you realize that the High Priest of your profession is closer to you than that at which you are looking? That is not very far away! He's nearer than that! He's abiding in your heart! And, the Lord, our God, in the center of our hearts, is mighty!

Now, look at the word, **"profession."** It means **"to agree with"** and it also means **"confession."**

Now, look at **Hebrews 4:14**. It speaks again of our Great High Priest, **"Seeing then that we have a great high priest, that is passed into the heavens, Jesus the Son of God, let us hold fast our *profession.*"** The word **"profession"** here is exactly the same word as in **Hebrews 3:1**. Here it means **"to agree with"** but with the addition of **"to say the same thing"**! Now of whom is the writer speaking here? He is speaking of Jesus Christ, Himself. We are to agree with the great High Priest of heaven Himself! The word, **"profession"** means that we are to say the same things that He says. I want this truth to build, and to expand, and to develop in your heart! It is essential for your faith to grow.

There is another scripture that is vitally important to this point: **Isaiah 55:11**. It has to do with the word, **"confession,"** which is another meaning of the word, **"profession."** There is something I want to share before we get into this verse.

There is a teaching that has been around for some time that tells you, all you have to do is to just confess it, and there it is. That is just one step away from Christian Science, and not a very long step at that. To just say it is not enough! However, there is enough truth in it, that it almost sounds real enough. You do not just "confess" something, and by that confession, create something out of nothing, because that is God's job.

I was invited to preach a revival in St. Louis a few years ago. When the pastor called, he told me that he had a group of people in his church who were all confessing that they had Cadillacs, but in fact, most were driving Volkswagens. He told me someone had come and told his people that all they had to do was just confess something and it would happen. It had not happened! I have watched sadly as people have written checks to pay for things when they did not have the money in the bank to cover their checks. They confessed that the money would be there when the checks came in, but then discovered they were overdrawn. That is not God's plan! That is not faith!

God has given us this wonderful truth in **Isaiah 55:11** which says **"So shall my word be that goeth forth out of my mouth: it shall not return unto me void, but it shall accomplish that which I please, and it shall prosper in the thing whereto I sent it."** God has given you and me the glorious privilege of being able to agree with everything Jesus our Lord has said. This is what we must confess. We must confess His Word. This is how we build our faith. These words in Isaiah are not just Isaiah's words. They are God's! They were not only true in 460 B.C., but they are true right now!

Jesus said in **John 17:8, "For I have given unto them the words which thou gavest me; and they have received them, and have known surely that I came out from thee, and they have believed that thou didst send me."** Jesus has given us words with which we can perfectly agree. He has given us the words of the Father.

Jesus, this very moment, is seated at the right hand of the Father, ever living to make intersession for us. **Hebrews 8:1** says **". . . We have such an high priest, who is set on the right hand of the throne of the Majesty in the heavens."** While He sits there, He waits for our outpoured prayers.

There is another teaching in the world today that you no longer need to pray, that all you need to do is "claim it." This teaching tells us that all we have to do is just speak, and that that which we say will come to pass. **Prayer has always been essential!** That, my friends, will never change! Look at Jesus praying, praying, praying. Daniel fasted and prayed for 21 days before his answer came. Prayer becomes the key to heaven, but it takes faith to unlock the door.

Why should Jesus have to sit at the right hand of the Father to make intersession for the saints, if you and I were not to pour out our petitions to Him? But, as our Lord sits there making intercession for us, for what is He waiting? Do you think He is waiting to hear how awful our problem is? He knows our problems better than we know them. Do you think He is waiting for us to tell Him how badly we feel about our need? We can be assured that there are many aching hearts! We would be amazed at how many aching hearts there are in the world today. But, we can't tell Him anything He doesn't already know. You see, He's touched by the feelings of our infirmities, **Hebrews 4:15** says **"For we have not an high priest which cannot be touched with the feeling of our infirmities: but was in all points tempted like as we are, yet without sin."**

What is He waiting for as He sits on the throne? He is waiting for us to take the Word He has given us and send it back to Him in prayer! He is waiting for us to say the same thing He has said. We must come to Him and say, "Jesus, I agree with what you say!" The Lord is my **"profession."** That is the heart of the **"confession"** ministry.

When we come to the throne, no matter what promise we are bringing before Him, we're bringing it back to the starting point. That's what He means in **Isaiah 55:11**, when He says, **" . . . my word shall not return unto me void."** When that promise comes back to its starting point, God knows, by your words, that you have agreed with Him! That's the reason that **"faith"** is not a thing or a noun. Faith is operative—it's an action! When we have seen the promise and say, "Lord, I agree with that. I send it back. I believe it, just like you have said it!" then, His word does not return unto Him void. It accomplishes the work for which it was sent! Can you see how faith is involved in all of this? Jesus wants us to agree with His Word from the beginning to the end.

To agree with what He has said, is to believe, and to believe, is to exercise faith! To have faith is to please God! Faith is what moves mountains! Faith will move mountains in your life!